Social Media Marketing

Instagram Marketing
Facebook Marketing

Table of Contents

Book 1: Instagram Marketing

Step by Step Guide on Instagram Advertising. How to Promote and Sell Anything through Instagram

Introduction

The internet and digital media have paved the way for a world of opportunities. It is a world where you can sell anything so long as you have the right idea and desire to make cash.

With the advent of Instagram and other channels of social media, anyone can create a brand and make themselves known. You can advertise your business, products, and services and become a leader in your field. However, the sad news is that you can't get the success you desire just by posting appealing images. No, it goes beyond that, and there are a lot of things you need to learn to ensure this. Nonetheless, this does not mean it is far from your reach.

In the chapters to follow, you will learn all there is to know about Instagram. You will learn what Instagram is, why it is vital for your brand, and how to create a good business account. This is not all; you will also learn the best software for scheduling posts and how to make money via Instagram among a range of others.

More importantly, you will learn to create Instagram ad campaigns for the best reach and use stories and contests to help you sell your products and services to your audience. This and many more are what we will break down in this book.

I do not promise you that it will be an easy task. Attaining success on Instagram is not without its problems. However, I am confident that when you are through with this book, you will have detailed knowledge of how to be successful on Instagram.

Researching this book has been fun to do. I hope you will find it entertaining and easy to understand while reading.

Now, let us begin this fantastic journey.

Chapter 1
Instagram Basics

At some point, you may have come across the name Instagram. This is most likely the case even if you have no active profile. That is just how recognized Instagram has become today. One of the major perks of Instagram are the various photo filters, which when used on a typical image, makes it seem like it was professionally edited. There are filters which can make your pictures black and white, while others can boost the colors in the photos.

Although Instagram filters transformed editing on mobile devices for many of us, that is not all it has to offer. This application has a user base of more than 50 million! Remarkable right? What's more, it was able to attain this feat while on Android and iOS devices. When Instagram kicked off, in just six days, there were more than 4 million downloads! (Taylor, 2012).

The success of the app drew the attention of one of the most recognized social platforms in the globe: Facebook. On the 9th of April, Instagram was acquired for $1 billion by Facebook. Instagram has covered a lot of ground in terms of business since its introduction in 2010(Price, 2012). However, the app remains one of the easiest to use to date.

If you are not yet on Instagram, it is not a problem. In this chapter, we will be learning all the essentials to ensure you can set yourself up and get things running. But first, let's look further into Instagram.

What Is Instagram?

Instagram is a platform for social networking, which was designed around the sharing of videos and photos. It was initially kicked-off on iOS in October 2010. In April 2012, it was released for Android devices.

Similar to a majority of social media applications, Instagram gives you the capacity to follow individuals you have an interest in. When you do this, it develops a feed on your homepage where you can see recent posts from those you follow. You will also have the capacity to comment on posts and like them. Instagram also offers support for Stories, which is similar to Snapchat. With Stories, you can post a picture or set of images and video clips. These will be visible to others for a 24hour period before it expires and vanishes.

Additionally, Instagram lets you send direct messages to others privately. You can also check out their profiles to view things that interest you. So how does Instagram work? We will be learning how below, but first, you need to learn to create an account.

Creating an Instagram Account

The first step to take when it comes to creating an Instagram account is to download the application. If you use an Android phone, head to the Google Play store. If you are an iOS user, check out the App store. In any of these stores, run a search and instantly download.

After you have downloaded the application, you can now begin. All you have to do is select the camera icon. For those who don't want to download the app, there is not a problem. You can open Instagram on your desktop. However, there is a limitation to the number of actions you can perform on your desktop as opposed to your mobile device. Now that you have covered this, the next step is to sign up.

Sign Up

It is mandatory for you to provide some information before you sign up. However, you are privy to a few choices which we will cover below:

- **Offer Your Mobile Number**: Here, you need to input your number, and you will be on your way to creating your account. If this is your first time of using the platform, this may be the ideal method of signing up. This info will always be accessible to you, and it will be less challenging to log in.

- **Use an Email Address**: If you already have an account on Instagram, this might be a good option for you, since you will be able to utilize a different email address. Receiving notifications is also seamless if you have more than one account, and you want to keep them separate.

- **Sign-up using Facebook**: For those who already have an account on Facebook, this is a fast and straightforward method of signing up and finding those you know who are already on Instagram. You will get immediate access to your list of friends, and you will be able to see those who are on Instagram. This makes it less difficult to follow those you know.

All of these methods can help you sign up with ease, so all you need is to choose the one that suits you best. After signing up, you can then move to the next step of picking a username.

Choose a Username

The username you choose is a very vital aspect of creating a new account on Instagram. Picking an account name can be very unnerving for many, but don't forget that it is something you can change any moment you want.

Knowing this, usernames are a very vital aspect of Instagram. A good name can help make your account unique and even help increase your follower count. The name you choose is dependent on what the account is for. As a rule of thumb, select a username that people can search for with ease. We will be taking a more in-depth look into usernames further in this book.

Select a Profile Picture

After you have carefully picked a username, now you need a picture on your profile. If it is an account for personal use, pick a great selfie. If your account is for business, choose one that explains what you do. If you like, you can also go with graphics. The idea is to use something you are comfortable with.

Any picture you decide to go with will be what users see first. Anytime you make an upload on Instagram, your profile picture will be right beside it. For this reason, you need to be careful when choosing a profile picture. Having selected your ideal profile picture, you can now follow those you know.

Start Following Those You Know

After putting your new account in place, it's time to start using Instagram. Look for the accounts of your friends and other accounts that you may have an interest in and begin to hit the follow button.

Ensure those you share a relationship with know that you now have an Instagram profile. The instant you begin to follow people; you will certainly get a follow back. In no time, you will have a successful Instagram account. Now that you have created your account, we will be looking into how it works, to ensure you can easily find your way around the platform.

Instagram- How Does It Work

After you have signed up and followed individuals, as we explained above, your Home tab will become quite active. Here, you will view posts from individuals and friends you have followed. Above, you will be able to see new stories uploaded by your friends. With a single tap, you can begin viewing the stories.

To send a direct message to other users, you can select the **Messages** icon. Tap it to begin a new message or check out the messages you presently have.

Making Posts on Instagram

To add a new post, all you need to do is to hit the **Plus** icon which you can find at the center of the toolbar beneath. Here, you can decide to take a new video or picture. You can also pick one image from your gallery or include many photos in a single post.

Once you have taken your picture, you can use one of the various filters offered by Instagram to edit your photographs. Lastly, you can include a comment to your uploads, tag those you know, include the locations if you desire, and decide if you want to send your uploads to other social platforms. The instant you hit the **Share** button, your picture will show up on your profile and the feeds of your followers. However, if you understand how to make posts on Instagram, and don't know the features at your disposal, you may not be able to take advantage of all the platform has to offer.

Features of Instagram

Instagram has included tons of features since its inception, which can be of benefit to marketers. Below are a few of the important ones that you have at your disposal.

Video Features

Similar to the typical photos posts, Instagram offers a video post feature. These video uploads are 60 seconds long. You can include a caption and filter. You can also tag your location before you upload the post.

In contrast to photos, video posts draw in more engagement from users. For brands or individuals who want to get ahead of the new Instagram algorithm which leverages the user engagement of your posts to decide if to show your content of the feed of users or not, this can offer huge potential.

Live Video

Live video has a concept which is different from the video posts. However, it is a fantastic feature to take advantage of. Here, followers are sent a push notification which informs them that you are about to go live. If followers click on the notification, they are redirected to your live video stream where they can like or leave comments in real time.

However, the instant you end the live stream, the video vanishes. For marketers looking to develop brand uniqueness and transparency, which are both vital on Instagram now, this is another effective method.

Mute Accounts

This feature allows you to mute post notifications from accounts of your choice. It is convenient in situations where you don't want to unfollow the said account. Also, this feature can help you keep up with your top accounts without any disruptions from accounts you don't want to view. It offers you control over the posts that show up on your feed.

IGTV

Instagram TV is an application you can find on Instagram. It offers users the capacity to share videos that are up to 60 minutes in length –similar to a TV episode. This can be very useful for individuals involved in video content creation which is one of the fastest rising innovations in content marketing, as more than 80 percent of businesses have begun tapping into the viability of video marketing.

Emoji Slider Polls

Now, you can use emojis to run polls. This new feature allows you to use emojis to let users take a poll on something they like or dislike.

If you are a marketer, there are a host of possibilities to this. You can upload an upcoming product in various colors and ask users to give it a rating. That way, you will know what the users want even before you decide to release. Doing this can save businesses a considerable amount of costs.

Stories

Like we covered above, the stories feature shares many similarities to Snapchat. Lots of users enjoy using stories which have led to a lot of updates. Below are some of the various ways you can use stories.

- **Mention Other Users**: Now, you can mention or tag other users in your stories. Just use the @ to find whomever you want to tag. You can integrate the mentions to stories or include them on the images. It can be used in tagging locations or those you know. When you are tagged by another user in their stories, you will get notified via your DM, and you will then have the capacity to upload the user's story as well.

- **Add Shoppable Tags to Stories**: Do you sell products or services? With this feature, you can tag your products in your stories. For instance, say you sell basketball shorts —you will tag the shorts in your stories so users can click and make direct purchases. This can help advertise your products in a user-generated or live action content.

- **Upload More Than One Story**: Now, you can upload videos and photos in bulk to your stories. If you are a marketer or social media marketer, this can save you tons of time as you will be able to upload ten images or videos simultaneously.

The features above are only a few of what Instagram offers. Take advantage of them today and make your marketing efforts more effective. Knowing these, let's delve into some of the other benefits you stand to gain from using Instagram for marketing.

Benefits of Instagram for Marketing

Instagram offers tons of perks to marketers, businesses, and individuals alike. Below are some of these fantastic benefits:

Lots of Individuals Are Utilizing Instagram

Instagram presently has more than 800 million active users, which is a massive amount if you look at it from a business perspective. From these millions of individuals, more than 50 million use the platform each day, with over 70 percent of them in other locations besides the United States (Balakrishnan & Boorstin, 2017). What's more, millennials make 34 percent of this number, and 38 percent of these visitors visit the site more than once every day (Clarke, 2019). With the vast amount of users, a business with the right Instagram strategy can attain colossal success.

Various Businesses Can Flourish

With access to this vast number of users, businesses are provided with infinite possibilities. This applies to established organizations as well as one-man companies. However, even for companies that are highly recognized, success is not an overnight task. Nonetheless, if a marketing team has the right strategy and is serious about getting visibility for their business, it is not impossible. They can make this happen by retaining an active presence on Instagram and posting at least once each day. This is the same way recognized brands like Adidas and Coca-Cola have attained vast levels of success using Instagram ("Social Media Case Studies & Client Stories | Sprout Social", 2019).

You Can Make Money On Instagram

Instagram has undergone many changes over the years. Now, more emphasis is placed on earning cash using product placement. With the shoppable posts, you can include tags to your products in uploads with links consisting of the price, product description and the capacity to make a purchase using the 'shop now' button, which directs users to your eCommerce store.

Using this easy feature, you can use the Instagram platform to get real sales. More than 70 percent of the users on Instagram stated that they purchased products via the platform, which makes it something worth taking advantage of (Smith, 2019).

It offers Stories

Instagram offers you the opportunity to let prospective clients know that there is a face behind your brand. You can do this using one of the numerous features you can access on the application; however, to make a lasting impression, stories, and live posts can do the trick. By using stories to take users on a walk behind-the-scenes of your organization and the individuals you work with, you can make your brand more relatable. A way of doing this is to post videos that show the way products are created, live Q&A sessions between your audience and yourself, among others.

The live post feature offered by Instagram is also an excellent way for you to build trust, credibility, and trust with the individuals who follow you. It could also help your brand feel less robotic and show that your business has a more human side. If your clients can see that you are more than just a corporation in search of ways to get their money, then it can help build your trust with them.

Collaborate with Influencers

If you have not heard the term before, Influencers are individuals with huge reach and credibility online, that can raise your brand's awareness with ease.

A skilled influencer can help increase your organization's returns because they have access to a target market in your niche that you won't usually have. If you can collaborate with an established influencer, they can aid in spreading the word of your product, services, or organizations to millions of individuals with only a few posts.

You can Enhance your visibility with Hashtags

As a newcomer in a particular sector, your competition may rattle you. However, if you properly implement hashtags, you can make your business stand out from the others.

Hashtags are similar to keywords. They help explain the message your post is trying to pass across. Well-known hashtags like #ShareaCoke by Coca-Cola have made waves in the industry and have made it even easier to love and recognize these brands.

You don't have to be a massive brand like Coca-Cola, but if you can efficiently implement hashtags, it can make a massive difference in helping your business stand out.

Engaging with Customers is Easy

What better way can you ingrain your business in the mind of clients? How about the chance to interact with them daily? Individuals love to air their opinions; it is a known fact, particularly if they like something.

Instagram is a channel for users to comment on, like, and share their top posts.

The higher the number of comments and likes you get; the more visibility your organization gets. Increasing your number of likes is straightforward too. You can do this by taking pictures of high-quality, collaborating with other similar brands and using hashtags.

It is Mobile

In contrast to other platforms like Twitter and Facebook, which launched as sites based on browsers, Instagram began as an application from the beginning. Since over 80 percent of the time individuals spend on mobile is used on apps, your organization can exploit this and ensure your viewers can access your posts with ease on the move anywhere they are through Instagram.

People who use smartphones prefer Instagram because it does not have the disorderly view Facebook tends to have. Also, you will want to exploit this because it has been reported that Instagram engagement is more than ten times that of Facebook. This is undoubtedly a wide margin that can make a lot of difference to your marketing efforts.

Monitor the Competition

Your organization can watch its competition with the help of Instagram and observe the way they relate with the individuals who follow them. Observe carefully to learn the frequency at which they post, the content they post and how they relate with their followers. You can use what you learn to better define your strategy, and stay ahead of the competition.

It Provides You with Numerous Ways to Be Creative

Instagram offers you the opportunity to get creative. On Instagram, you can try out various strategies to come up with new ways to attract attention and add new customers and followers. You can prove to your followers that there is a personality behind your brand, and shopping with you can be a great experience. You can do this by combining shoutouts, contests, interactive videos, and vivid images, among others.

Link with Facebook

As we covered earlier, Instagram was purchased by Facebook for a whopping sum of $1 billion. For businesses who want to combine their marketing efforts on both platforms, this purchase came with a lot of opportunities.

Facebook and Instagram ads share a lot of similarities, and now that they are typically the same company, you can now run the same ad on Instagram and Facebook simultaneously. What this implies is that the instant you run an ad on any of these platforms, you can instantly double your reach.

Instagram Offers Great Analytics

With Instagram, measuring your success is very easy. Similar to other platforms, it allows you to keep track of your follower counts, levels of engagements, among others. However, Instagram takes it a little further by providing you with comprehensive analytic reports. These can aid you in interpreting the outcome of your ad campaigns with ease. With these analytics, you will be able to quickly pinpoint the kinds of posts on Instagram that offer the best results, so you can keep using them for continuous success.

It is a known fact that creating a new account on Instagram can be a scary process for many people. However, it can also be an enjoyable process, as well. Also, with the number of individuals taking advantage of this platform continually on the rise, you will be ignoring a massive amount of prospective clients if you are not on this platform. Start building your brand today, and you will have no regrets you did. What if you have no brand yet and want to begin? We will be exploring how you can do this in the next chapter.

Chapter 2
Creating Your Instagram Brand

Almost anyone can develop a brand on Instagram nowadays. However, developing a memorable brand that users would want to follow is something much more complex. This, on its own, is a technique that needs to be learned.

In this chapter, we will cover how to create a memorable brand for yourself on Instagram. Below are the steps that can help:

Define Your Objectives

The first thing you need to do even before making any post is to determine the reason you want to build your brand on the platform.

What are your objectives? What do you plan to achieve using Instagram?

Do you want to:

- Spread brand awareness?

- Find new clients?

- Try to build a community?

- Connect with existing customers?

- Enhance traffic to your blog?

- Enhance your impression on social media?

Depending on the type of brand you wish to build, your goals and objectives can differ. However, you can alter your goals as you grow.

Determine your Focus

After establishing your objectives, the next step is to determine your theme or focus on Instagram. Many brands make the error of having no focus and make random posts on Instagram. This will fail because you won't be able to make yourself unique from the others.

Locate a focus that aligns with your personality and stick to it. Your focus should also align with your brand. Try to have a direction from the start; your goal should be to let your followers know you and the services you offer. If you are at a loss as to what theme to be, all you need to do is get inspiration from Instagram by running a search. There are a lot of amazing accounts which will inspire you.

Define Your Theme

Your theme is your style on Instagram. It is one you stick with all through the time you use Instagram. Some users stick with a neutral only style, while some would prefer a darker style. For others, they choose to include funny posts after every three posts. If you want to be unique, its best to combine things a bit.

Consistently Release High-Quality Content

Posting frequently on social media platforms is essential, and the same applies to Instagram. If you desire to be unique, you need to publish content often.

To make things easier, you can use a tool to schedule posting as we covered in the previous chapter. As a rule of thumb, it is best to have content that would last you for no less than two weeks in place, before you begin. If you have new content you want to post, you can push it ahead in your scheduling tool.

Stay Active

To have a great brand on Instagram, you have to build a community. You can only do this if you are active.

Easy ways of doing this include:

- Commenting on the profile of others

- Following other people

- Liking the pictures of other users

These may seem basic, but it is a strategy that is certain to provide results.

Leverage Hashtags

To have the most impact, you have to take advantage of hashtags. If you can, take advantage of all 30 hashtags. If you are unaware of the hashtags to utilize, you can check out what your competitors or established influencers in your field are using.

It is vital to use hashtags because it offers exposure when individuals are going through hashtags to view pictures.

Develop a Branded Hashtag

A branded hashtag is one that you create for yourself. Putting one in place is a fantastic way to develop engagement instantly. A branded hashtag is when users utilize your hashtag to get an opportunity to feature on your Instagram account.

Many users enjoy tagging pages and utilizing hashtags on Instagram to be featured on a specific page. It is an excellent means of getting more followers and exposure.

The first step is to state it on your profile that anyone who uses your hashtag will get featured on your page. Then, look for a hashtag which is a bit popular with lower than 50k posts, head to those pictures and begin to like them. It is an excellent way of ensuring people notice your page. This will urge your followers and the individuals whose pictures you liked, to post images using your hashtags in a bid to feature on your page.

Reuse Content Published by Other Accounts

This is another excellent option if you don't want to utilize branded hashtags. Look for posts that are similar to your style and repost them on your page. In doing this, you can increase engagement and create connections with other users simultaneously.

To make sure the image quality is terrific, contact these individuals to get the authority to post their content on your account. Let them send you a picture of high-quality. This way, you get a good picture while creating connections too.

Search for Branded Accounts and Hashtags

If you want exposure, an effortless way is to locate accounts or branded hashtags in the same industry as you to get featured on.

An easy way of doing this is to run a search for a popular hashtag your demographic uses, and find out if they have used or tagged any hashtags to get a feature.

If you share how-to's on your account, you are not alone. Numerous accounts share how-to's from others. Keep an eye out for them. To go further, you can contact them via their Instagram DM to get them to notice you.

Collaborate with Other Accounts

A great way of branding your account and growing it at the same time is to collaborate with accounts that have similar engagement and following as yours. It is also recognized as a shoutout for shoutout.

This typically works this way; When you make a post, on the caption you put something in the lines of "If you want more amazing pictures like this, follow this account @user."

The account you are collaborating with also does the same thing, and you both get followers who are interested in what you do.

How to Choose a Great Instagram Name?

Determining the best Instagram username can be very complex; however, it is quite significant. It portrays the identity you are trying to pass along and also presents your content

These steps below can aid you in selecting an Instagram name that is simple, unique, appealing, and available.

Determine Your Context

When it comes to picking an Instagram username, a very vital step is to determine what you plan on doing with your Instagram account. Are you developing a personal Instagram page to post images of exotic locations you visit? Or are you picking a username for your business or blog? You need to determine what your plan is before you can effectively choose an Instagram username.

Pick the Components

If your goal is to post personal pictures for your family and loved ones to see, you may want to include the following components: first name, middle, and last name. You also want to add any nickname you might have alongside your date of birth.

If your goal is to create an account for your business, you may want to integrate your business name, the kind of business, the business location, and the keywords common in its field. Using the same username on all your business social media pages is a great idea. The instant you choose a username, ensure that is the same one you use for Twitter, Facebook, and if possible, your email.

Mix Things Up

Having determined the components, you want to incorporate in your user name, try to shake things up to see which of the arrangement seems better. You want to go with a username that is not difficult to remember, sounds great when read aloud and looks great when typed out. For a business Instagram username, it is especially critical to pick one that is easy to remember. Don't pick one with many numbers because users would likely not recognize. Also, make sure you don't use any information that can be used to identify you, like your address or phone number. You don't want random users on Instagram to begin ringing up your line because you uploaded it on Instagram.

Other Things to Avoid

Avoid underscores. Finding this symbol on the keyboard can be so tedious. Also, when you use more than one underscore at the same time, it can be hard to point out the numbers.

Don't copy the Instagram username of another user with only one letter being different. Users would be unable to tell you apart, and that user may not find this appealing.

Ensure it is not too lengthy. It is difficult to type out or remember lengthy usernames. Use something memorable and brief.

Check If your Chosen Username Is Available

After you have selected a few usernames, you need to check if they are available. You can use a tool for this or run a search for the username to determine if there is a username similar to it. If it is not available, you can use punctuation. Instagram supports punctuation differences, and they can sometimes make your handle more legible.

You have the luxury to try as many usernames as possible. And the instant you have determined your component, there are a host of combinations you can use. The moment you have a few options that you have proven to be available, you can say them out loud and pick the best sounding one.

If it does not work out, and you go with a name you dislike, later on you can change it without any impact on your account. If you want to use another username, head to your profile, and hit "edit profile." When doing this, repeat the steps from the start and experiment with new usernames. Also, remember to find out if these names are in use. You don't want to pick a name and learn later that it is in use.

If you have a great brand, but your profile/bio is in a mess, you may never get the reach you desire. This makes it a vital reason to learn to create a good bio that attracts people. The next chapter will cover this in more detail.

Chapter 3
How to Create A Great Bio

Many individuals who use Instagram for marketing tend to make the mistake of ignoring their profile/bios. For the ones who do remember, their bio is something they fill in a rush when they create their accounts.

However, this should not be the case. Your bio is a significant aspect of your page, which is the first thing visitors see. It passes vital information regarding your business, establishes a great first impression for your business and transforms individuals who visit your profile into visitors and ultimately, customers.

For this reason, you need to understand how to make your profile catchy and appealing as this will help you get the best from your account on Instagram alongside your efforts in marketing. What else can you do? That is what we will be covering in this chapter. First, we will be looking at the basics.

Instagram Bio – What is it?

Your Instagram bio, like we covered earlier, aids in describing you and your business. It is the first thing visitors come across. Instagram offers you 150 characters to utilize in your bio. Also, you will be allowed to add one external link. There is also additional input for your username, which has an extra 30-character length. With this in mind, what does your bio have to achieve?

What Should Your Instagram Bio Achieve?

There are a lot of things your profile/bio should accomplish. They may seem like a lot considering you are restricted to a specific number of characters. Nonetheless, a great Instagram bio has to cover the following:

- Show vital information about your business, like the name of your brand, industry, and so on. You can change this at any time via your profile settings.

- Offer users on Instagram with a means of reaching you.

- Display the personality of your brand, ensuring your style and voice aligns with your website and any other social platforms you may have.

- Determine your unique selling point, to aid your target audience, interpret why your brand is relevant to them

- Push relevant actions like viewing or sharing content, heading to the website to buy a product, leave a comment, or follow back.

The good news is that Instagram offers you a range of features that you can utilize along with your bio. With these features, you can easily cover the essential profile considerations, which will aid users in understanding your business and what you do, to enable you take additional steps.

Now, we will be taking a look at how to make an exceptional Instagram bio.

Take Advantage of Keywords

If you hit "Edit Profile", "Name" is the first area you will find. It is not the same as your Username, which is what creates the URL of your Instagram profile. It offers your page its name.

The initial 30 characters of your bio is made up of the name field, and it can go a long way in your Instagram SEO efforts. When individuals run a search for something on Instagram, it analyzes the words used in the Name field for a fit. So if your goal is to have a good ranking when it comes to Instagram SEO, you need to take advantage of keywords that are significant to your niche by including them in the Name field. If you can, try to include emojis in the Name field as people tend to run a lot of searches on them.

Writing Your Bio

Your Instagram bio hugely affects your audience. From a glance, people should be able to understand what your business is all about and why they are relevant to you. The bio should also have the capacity to lure people to follow you, and finish a specific action you desire like follow a website, or make a purchase.

You need to try to fit in as much data as you can, concerning your brand in the allocated 150 characters. This can be a tedious task considering the tight character limit. Due to this, we will be covering some of the vital information that should be included in your bio;

- Precise Service or Niche: If you belong to a particular industry niche or profession, or you are known to provide a specific service, then it is vital to make this evident in your Instagram bio so you can connect instantly with the appropriate crowd.

- Experience and Skills: By letting your audience know your level of expertise and what you can do, it will be easy to build trust with them, while providing them with a look into the services you render.

- Interests and Hobbies: If your brand is dependent on you as a person, then it is vital for you to develop a connection with your audience. Tell them a little about your interests, who you are, beliefs, and values so you can present yourself as engaging and captivating.

- Add a little humor to your brand's voice: It is vital to use the voice of your brand, as doing this will make sure you stay consistent on every social network and allow your audience to recognize you instantly. However, including a bit of humor will make it easier to relate to your brand.

You need to consider a host of things when you are putting together your Instagram bio. However, there are a lot of things you need to incorporate. Below are a few other components you need to add to develop a great bio

Take Advantage of Hashtags

Including a branded hashtag in your bio is another essential Instagram technique. In addition to creating a community for your brand, it will also aid you in driving post engagement. For instance, Airbnb efficiently utilizes its branded hashtag in its bio and even uses it to urge user-generated content.

When you offer your followers the means to distribute their content with your community using your branded hashtag, it will be less challenging to develop an engaging Instagram page. This can aid you in promoting your company and ensuring your brand gets to a broader audience.

Include Emojis

A great way to give your profile an exciting and authentic look, while ensuring your brand is unique, is to include emojis.

What's more, emojis don't require the same character counts words do. This means you will be able to include additional information concerning your brand, which would have been impossible if you were using text.

Below are a few ways to utilize emojis in your bio:

- Try combining a few words with emojis. Feel free to be creative about this.

- Utilize emojis to draw attention to your content's key point. You can also utilize them as bullet points to separate texts and make them less difficult to read

- Any emojis you add to your bio should relate to what you do and should enhance your bio.

- Using emojis without any accompanying texts is not advisable. It may confuse your audience, and in doing this, you are just wasting space you could have used for something vital.

Also, note that you can be creative with your use of emojis. Toy with various emojis to determine the most suitable for your brand.

Website URL: Including A Link in Your Bio

Instagram only gives you the chance to include one clickable link, which comes up beneath your bio. Many Instagram users showcase the URL of their site's homepage, which is a smart move if you want to push more traffic to your website.

But, if your Instagram and your business objectives change along the line, you need to also change your URL link to support the new goal. You can include a link to your recent blog post or marketing campaign. There are a ton of options available for you to exploit here, so ensure you get the best from your link in your Instagram bio by letting it align with the objectives of your business.

CTA or Call to Action

An ideal location to include a call to action or CTA is your Instagram bio. Let your audience know the action you want them to take, and if you can, how to go about it.

For instance, request that they follow you on other platforms. If you have a product, you can also ask that they make a purchase. If you have a physical address for your business, you can include it in your bio alongside your opening and closing times, to ensure people can locate you and visit you with ease. Besides, you can request that your followers open a specific web page, by including the URL in the space allocated for a website.

Pick a Profile Image

This is the last step of the process. You need to pick a great profile picture, and the ideal choice is to go with your brand logo, which is already in use on your other social media platforms and website. When you use a symbol that is easy to identify, it will make it easier for your target audience to find you. It will also aid in elevating your brand awareness by ensuring it is visible on social media within your niche market.

A great Instagram brand bio consists of a range of components. However, you are allowed to be flexible and creative with this. Try numerous texts, calls to actions, and emojis. By frequently changing your Instagram bio, you will learn what triggers a response from your audience, and what functions for your organization.

The next step after ensuring your bio is as great as it can be, is to choose the right niche to focus on. We will be viewing how to go about this in the next chapter.

Chapter 4
Choosing the Right Niche

You have learned how to make posts of Instagram; you also understand why a name is vital. You have even created a great brand and bio, and so you begin to post random, high-quality content. You sit back and wait for the likes and comments to come in as your followers grow because you have done everything right.

However, you don't see any progress. Not many people aside from those you follow seem to have any interest in your posts. The issue may not be with what you are posting, but the way you post them. There is a range of individuals on Instagram using it effectively for their marketing needs. This is because they understand how the platform works and have learned to use it to their benefit for the best result.

One thing lots of marketers use to make themselves stand out is picking a niche and staying consistent with it. That way, they build themselves as authorities in that niche and are the first ones that come to the minds of users when they think of anything that relates to that niche. Knowing this, we will be covering everything about choosing a niche and making yourself stand out on Instagram in this chapter. But first, what is a niche?

What Is a Niche?

We may keep hammering on you choosing the right niche, but the truth is, if you don't know what a niche is, you won't even know where to begin.

A niche market is typically a part of a broader market. Similar to a slice of pizza. For instance, a market could be games, while niches within that consist of PS4 games, Xbox games, PC games, and so on. You can narrow it down a little further by saying PS4 sports games, Xbox adventure games, etc. When you define your niche market, it implies that you have a clear understanding of your target market and all the vital information, what they require, and how you can make it available for them.

Choosing a niche ensures it is less challenging to target, promote, and deliver. Why invest time marketing PS4 games to users who have a passion for Xbox games only? In addition to helping you target with ease, a niche can help you make lots of profit and save you the cash you would have used in marketing to the wrong audience. When choosing a niche market, you don't just pick the first subject that comes to mind, or you may never go far. There is a right way to choose a niche, which we will cover below.

How to Pick a Niche Market?

People should know your Instagram page for a specific thing. This may be any topic you have an interest in, which could range from mobile phones to footwear. Any niche you choose must be one you are passionate about and can make endless posts on without getting bored.

If you are having problems narrowing down your niche, you can search Instagram a bit deeper. Go through the best pages that have to do with subjects that interest you. Know the individuals in that field, and the hashtags that are typically used with that specific subject.

Choosing a niche for yourself should be less complicated the instant you know if the niche has a presence on Instagram or not. Now, the next step is to determine your audience.

Determine Your Audience

After deciding what you will be posting about, you need to determine the individuals you will be speaking to online. To resolve this, ask yourself these questions:

- Who are my customers or audience?

- What value can I offer with my interests?

- What kind of content will I have the capacity to offer?

- How much engagement do I want?

- How much traffic can I conveniently handle each month?

The reason for these questions is to determine your customers so you can structure your content to prove to them they have an interest in the same things you do. If people can relate to your posts, they will follow you with ease. If you are in the dog niche, you can focus your content on dog care, dog leashes, best dog breeds, tutorials, etc.

The value you provide your community is vital because it lets your followers know your posts are relevant, and it will help them decide if they will keep seeing your posts or ignore them. The instant users know that they can get the most recent and accurate information about their favorite niche; you will soon become an authority and have a consistent flow of audience.

Develop a Strategy

Now that you have determined your niche and your audience, the next thing to do is to develop a strategy. If you are beginning, it is ideal to pick a niche and remain in that niche to increase the number of followers you have. An easy way of doing this is to follow individuals who share some similarities with your account and have the same interests.

Also, you will want to leave witty comments on their posts anytime they drop something new. The more you engage with the community, the higher the possibility of you gaining followers from there too. With time, they will also engage with your posts by commenting, liking, or sharing them. This is the point your content becomes vital. You want to ensure your content is informative and supported by videos and pictures to prove that you are providing the community with value. With time, the number of followers you have will increase and perhaps feature on the pages of others. When you develop a good strategy, it gives you the chance to interact with other pages efficiently.

Remain Steady

The instant you have increased your follower count; you need to remain consistent with your posts. When you post is vital, but you need to remember that what you post is more critical. If you go a week without any posts, with time, your followers will begin to forget you. To determine how frequently you should post, you can take a look at similar pages and see what they do. If they post two times a week, you need to post four times. If they make posts every 3-4 days, it's best to make yours daily until you grow more prominent instead of mirroring what they do. Remain consistent and leave posts that are relevant to your audience.

Ensuring You Have a Profitable Niche

You need to understand that not all niches offer the same kind of returns. Although you want to pick something you have a passion for, you still need a niche that will bring you adequate returns. It is not impossible to pick a niche that is not narrow enough.

For a niche to be profitable, it requires adequate numbers. To determine this, ask yourself the following:

- Are there sufficient individuals who have an interest in it to amass revenue consistently?

- Are people keen on spending their funds in the niche?

- Will you be able to provide a solution to a need, want, or problem for them?

- Can you enhance on a currently existing solution?

If your response to these questions is yes, then your niche is a profitable one. Nonetheless, you can try out other niches, mainly if you aim to make a profit in the long run. That being said, below are some of the most profitable niches you can choose on Instagram.

Profitable Niches on Instagram

There are a lot of niches that become popular for a while and phase out. Taking advantage of what is presently in vogue is not a terrible idea, but you never can tell when it will vanish. A better option is to find a subject in markets that are always profitable.

These are niches, or markets that are will always remain fresh, trendy, and popular years down the road. Below are a few of these niches:

Health and Fitness

Health and fitness services, products, content, and tools will always be in high demand. Most individuals take their health seriously, be it emotional, mental, physical, or otherwise to a reasonable extent.

You can provide hacks, tricks, or tips for people to stay healthy. You can also share your journey to wellness, fitness, or health. Also, you can suggest services and products which you produced or that of others. There is always a broad audience in the health and fitness niche, and they can never get enough. A few of the most recognized niches in this market include weightlifting, basketball, football, yoga, and cycling, among others.

Travel

Many of us imagine ourselves taking adventures in luxury locations. There is often a particular country or area we would love to check-out. In 2017, the travel industry had a value of $5.29 trillion, which makes it a very viable sector to tap into ("How much is the travel industry worth? Try US $5.29 trillion - Travelweek", 2019).

However, because this is a prevalent market, you need to narrow down your niche to the fullest if you want to have an effect on the market. Suggest and review locations to eat, places to stay, various cities, ways to move around in specific cities and fantastic videos and pictures for individuals in niches for outdoor enthusiasts, business travelers, and backpackers among others.

Beauty

The beauty market audience consists of mostly women, but there are also men that find it appealing, and it is not fading away any time soon.

It has been estimated that by 2024, the cosmetics industry will get to $863 billion ("Global Cosmetic Products Market Will Reach USD 863 Billion by 2024: Zion Market Research", 2019).

The #Beauty has more than 200 million posts associated with it, and the number is growing continuously. Sharing product reviews, tutorials, and how-to's is a great way to begin. And because beauty has a lot to do with visuals, it is a perfect fit for Instagram, which has 50.3 percent, female users ("Global Instagram user age & gender distribution 2019 | Statistic", 2019). A few of the top niches in the beauty market include makeup, skincare, hair, and nails.

Business

Money is essential for almost every individual. If you are well-versed in things that have to do with business, then tapping into the business niche is a great way to go. Perhaps you are a business coach who offers services that are vital to business owners like PR or marketing, or a business consultant who aids owners of businesses.

With numerous business owners presently on Instagram, this is undoubtedly a niche you will want to take advantage of. As usual, you need to focus, so don't try to generalize your niche. Rather, narrow it down and do it well. Offer tricks, how-to's, and hacks which lots of individuals will find useful; and with time your followers will grow, filled with individuals who would be willing to patronize you when you have something to sell.

Some of the most popular niches in this market include blogging, marketing, real estate, starting a business, and eCommerce, among others.

Fashion

This is a spin-off from the beauty market, however, it is a massive market on its own. Consider what is distinct about your style, then create a business along with a page on Instagram that portrays this style. Creating content will be very easy, considering you are just being yourself.

Also, it is not essential for you to be a professional fashion designer to tap into the fashion niche. Perhaps you understand how to develop the ideal look each day, or you have a still that is so distinct and appealing you turn heads anywhere you go. If your contact is unique and authentic, you will grab the attention of people quickly.

The following include some of the leading niches you can tap from in the fashion market: accessories, clothing, watches, and jewelry.

Lifestyle and Luxury

Everyone loves the good life and wishes to have a taste of it. If you enjoy taking pictures of cars, food, or your daily life, then this niche may be just what you need. The lifestyle niche has to do with you offering a look into the life that lots of people desire, regardless of if it is a life filled with positivity or that of a professional in a specific field.

The luxury niche, on the other hand, has to do with showing a glimpse of the life we all dream of. Notwithstanding the one you choose to go with, they are both very profitable and well-recognized. Some of the niches here include supercars, travel, and houses, among others.

Animals

In 2017, the pet sector amassed $86 billion in the United States (Schmidt, 2018). It has also been projected that pet care will surpass a worldwide estimate of $202 billion in the coming years ("Pet Care Market Size Worth $202.6 Billion By 2025 | CAGR: 4.9%", 2018). These include food, toys, pet insurance, treats, and clothing among a host of others.

Lots of men and women alike have a deep-rooted passion for animals and treat them like family. Tap into this love and enjoy the possibilities that come with it.

Relationships

There will always be relationship issues and drama in this world because everyone has them. For this reason, the relationship niche is a great one to exploit. Individuals are always in search of ways to understand the opposite sex, enhance their relationship among others. This means in this niche; you can gain a reasonable amount of following fast.

A few specific niches you can tap from in this market include parenting, business relationships, and friends. If you have tutorials and tips that can make it easy for people in relationships, then there is a lot of revenue to be made.

Gaming

Games are appealing to kids and even lots of adults. If you are close to someone who loves games, you most likely have an idea of how much games can be worth.

Individuals spend lots of money purchasing consoles, games, walkthroughs, and guides. Some of them even enjoy watching others review and play the most recent and expected games on YouTube and other platforms.

There are individuals on Instagram that make tons of cash playing and reviewing video games as a full-time job. One of these is the recognized

PewDiePie who has more than 14 million followers on Instagram. This niche is quite broad and still offers a lot of possibilities to newcomers.

Family/Parenting

This is another spin-off from the relationship market, but then this is a niche which is rising tremendously. Let's face it, being a parent is not easy and all new parents are always in search of advice to ensure they take all the right steps. Some want advice on products to purchase to make things easier. In 2018, the industry for baby care product was worth $73.86 billion (Johnson, 2019). Accounts focused on this niche appeal to lots of individuals because they can relate to it. Even if you have no kids, you indeed came from a family which makes it one of the more profitable niches you can find out there.

By now, you should have decided on your ideal niche. But even with the right niche, learning how to post high-quality content is still vital, or you won't get the kind of engagement you desire. The chapter below will delve deeper into this.

Chapter 5
Developing High-quality content on Instagram

For many individuals, creating content of high-quality can be a difficult task. Developing ideas and locating the appropriate visuals for your feed is easier in theory. In addition to being exciting and significant to your target audience, your content also has to look amazing.

Also, Instagram is a platform which is incredibly visual, and effective marketing campaigns rely heavily on engaging and appealing images. All of these combined increases the pressure to search for great content.

However, it does not have to be so tedious to create quality content on your Instagram account. There are a lot of techniques to use in creating high-quality content, and we will be taking an elaborate look at them in this chapter. But first, why do you need quality content on Instagram?

Benefits of High-Quality Content

To develop brand credibility and your target audience, you need to consistently make your content distinct. Before you advertise products or set up shoppable feeds, your content is what draws in the audience and transforms them into followers. Having quality content comes with a lot of benefits which include;

It Helps in Building Brand Loyalty

When it comes to the competitive field of social media, you only get one opportunity to make yourself stand out. With quality content, you can build trust and loyalty. A good way of attaining success on Instagram is to utilize the 80/20 rule. Offering value should be 80 percent of the time, while promotion should stay at 20percent.

Enhance Rate of Conversion

Contests, User-generated content, rewards, and CTs are types of contents that have a considerable possibility of enhancing your rates of conversions on Instagram. You can exploit all the opportunities offered by Instagram. For instance, even though hyperlinks are not allowed anywhere outside your bio, you can still take advantage of a CTA to urge your followers to take targeted action and transform them into prospective clients. Knowing these benefits, how then do you create high-quality content on Instagram? You will be learning this in the next section.

How to Develop High-Quality Content

As we have previously covered, Instagram is a social media channel which is based on visuals. This means the content you require to keep your audience engaged on Instagram has to do with Stories, videos, and photos. Before you make any post, the first step is to determine your objective.

What do you plan on accomplishing with your content? The following could be examples of some of your objectives:

- To promote an existing or new product

- To increase awareness for your business page or get more followers

- To draw in traffic to your website from your Instagram page

The instant you have put your objectives in place, the next thing you need to do is develop engaging content. Below are a few procedures to help you begin:

Find Out More about Your Audience

If you develop any content without knowing your audience, you may end up with the wrong kind of content. To learn about your audience, you need to determine the following:

- How do they utilize Instagram?

- What Instagram accounts do they have an interest in?

- Why are they on the platform?

To streamline things, you can carry out surveys or interviews with numerous individuals in your target group. This will help you determine their areas of needs and learn what is vital to them.

Think about Content with the Best Performance

Instagram has to do with images, but when it has to do with Instagram, you need to streamline your options. You need to share content that improves your visual presence and brings your brand utility to light.

You need to ensure you keep a narrative outline in all your images, so it can be easy to recognize you going forward. So what are the kinds of content you can share on Instagram? Below are some of your options:

- Share the beliefs and values of your organization

- Post pictures of your workplace. Give your followers the chance to create a connection with you and not only your service or product.

- Share Pictures of Individuals Utilizing Your Products

Even if you post the right kinds of content, if they do not align, then it may be challenging to succeed. This is why you need to develop patterns and themes for your content.

Develop Content Patterns and Themes

Having reviewed the expectations of your audience and what your goals are, you need to choose components of your brand, which you can emphasize via your Instagram content. Your services, team members, and brand products are all great places to begin for content themes. Next, think of topics that align with your stories, photos, and videos, and ensure the themes of your content go with your visuals. Even with a great theme, having poorly edited images or using random filters can affect the overall outcome of your content. This is why you need to learn to use filters the right way.

Learn to Use Filters

As stated by Canva (n.d.), the most utilized filter on Instagram is Clarendon. With this filter, you can highlight your images, brighten them, and also add shadows to make them appealing. Use a constant filter that tallies with the persona of your brand and offers it a consistent and distinct look.

According to a study carried out by Yahoo Labs and Georgia Tech, utilizing filters and including amazing copies to pictures could help enhance viewability by as much as 21 percent. It can also lead to a 45 percent enhancement in the number of comments (Friedman, 2015).

Exploit Hashtags

The main perks of hashtags is their capacity to ensure your content is more discoverable. In return, it grows your post engagement and audience. When categorizing content, Instagram capitalizes on hashtags. A good approach is to utilize them for the keywords you include in your copies.

To get the best from your content, you can try incorporating branded hashtags into each post. In doing so, you can link them to your brand, and oversee them with the aid of a tool for social media listening. There is no right amount when it comes to the number of hashtags you will be able to include in captions. However, it is vital to remain relevant and add hashtags that have to do with anything you post on Instagram. It is not ideal to fill your posts with irrelevant hashtags, all because you want more. Doing this can have a negative impact instead of the positive one you desire.

Pay attention to UGC Content

UGC means User Generated Content. It is a very efficient technique for raising your brand awareness on Instagram. UGC is when individuals who use a specific brand distribute its content with or without the brand motivating them.

If your brand is well-established and trusted, this approach would work well for you. But, if you are still making efforts to find a place for your brand online, no user will develop content regarding your brand without any encouragement or reward. For this reason, you need to run a promotional event or a contest where users would get a reward if they create and share content on your brand's behalf.

Cash in On Captions

Great visuals are a significant part of Instagram; however, it is also vital to have a productive caption. The reason is that it enhances comments and likes on your posts, and also drives engagement.

Instagram states that posts displayed in user feeds are presented based on the potential interest of the user in the content being offered. In simple terms, it implies that contents with a vast amount of comments and likes are better candidates to be presented at the top of the feed of your followers.

Instagram captions have the function of showcasing your brand's personality, entertaining your audience, and urging followers to take action. With captions, you can tell a moving story that will serve the final objective of your brand. There is no particular method of creating captions that work for everyone. Instead, the best option is for you to find what works for you.

Taking the captions on Nike's Instagram page, for example; some of their posts aim to inspire the audience while some are motivational. Take a cue from this and find out what works for you.

Repost Content from Brands Similar to Yours

What if you don't have the time to develop quality content for yourself? The great news is that it is not essential. If you are in a viable niche, there is a high possibility that there are other accounts consistently developing content that piques the interest of your audience.

It is not a bad idea to post content from Instagram bands that are similar to yours, or accounts that are significant to your Instagram strategy and followers, so long as you request authorization and appropriately credit the source.

To repost Instagram content, the right way, this what you have to do:

Follow Accounts and Hashtags to Find Content of High-Quality

To find the content you can repost, think of brands that have exhilarating Instagram accounts, which are not in direct competition with you, and have an audience similar to yours.

Take a look at their accounts and note the ones that create the leading contents you can share. Follow them so you can be notified about their new posts and save any particular posts you feel you can share on your page. You can easily do this by using the bookmark icon, which you can find underneath any video or post on Instagram. Better still, you can save the posts you plan on re-posting in a separate collection.

Another great way is to follow hashtags that are significant to your account. The excellent part of following hashtags is that posts linked to the hashtags you follow show up in your feed. This ensures it is less complicated for you to find fantastic content to repost. All you need to do is run a search for the hashtag on Instagram and follow!

Work with Influencers

If you want to get a continuous supply of quality content, working with influencers is a great way to go. This is because of their reasonable followers count. However, influencers are expensive, and if you have a limited budget, you can try working with a micro-influencer before you move to more recognized ones. When you collaborate with other micro-influencers in your niche, you will be able to reach around 10,000 to 40,000 individuals. This can be very significant if you work with influencers in the same niche as you. To contact influencers, you can send a DM or get their contact information from their bios.

Apps That Can Help You with Posting Content

As you must be aware, it can seem like a huge task to post content continuously. On average, many leading brands posts almost five times every week, which can consume numerous hours with ease. This is the reason lots of social media managers capitalize on applications that give them the capacity to load multiple contents and automate posting. Below are a few of the best apps that can help with posting and publishing content on Instagram.

Later

This is a platform established particularly for Instagram. This tool lets you schedule posts, monitor hashtags, and amass user-generated content among many others. Also, this app is an official partner of Instagram and utilizes their API for the importation of images, which makes it a very secure choice for organizations that are bothered about the safety of their social accounts.

Later does not cost anything for individuals, but you may need to pay some fees if you have a large company.

Buffer

Buffer is a scheduling application for social media, which is free of charge. You can integrate it with Instagram and a host of other recognized platforms on social media. With this application, you can post single images, and it also sends you reminders, to enable you posts videos manually and posts consisting of multiple images. This application is free for individuals but can be quite pricey for large brands with numerous users and accounts. Buffer comes as an iOS, web, and Android app.

Sprout Social

With Sprout Social, you can schedule posts on Instagram, manage comments, monitor hashtags, and run reporting. With this tool, you can schedule posts and automatically send them to Instagram. You can find this application online as a web app, Android, and iOS mobile application.

Hootsuite

Hootsuite is a very recognized platform for social media management. You can integrate it with all the core social networks apart from Instagram. With this application, you can automate posts and send reminders for posts. It is not as expensive as the competition, and you can use it as an iOS, Android, or web application.

Even if you develop the best content, posting it at the wrong time may not get you the traffic you want. You need to learn the right posting time for your content. We will be probing this more in the chapter to follow.

Chapter 6
Right Posting Time to Generate Buyers

Even when you upload the best content on your Instagram page, if you are posting at the wrong time on Instagram, you are setting yourself up to fail. The time you post on Instagram is just as crucial as the quality of content.

However, all brands may not have the same ideal posting time. Although there are studies which state that there are specific periods of the day that are typically better for posting, this practice may not suit your brand. It is a great place to start, but you will still have to try what works for you by using various posting times to determine the ideal one for your followers and your brand.

Similar to other social platforms, Instagram takes advantage of a continuously changing algorithm that makes things a little harder. If you have determined the best time for posting your contents, you still have to stay ahead of the changes to these algorithms by experimenting on, measuring, and improving your techniques. The Instagram algorithm takes note of the level of engagements attained by your post and how fast users interact with them, so you need to locate the ideal time to enhance your reach.

What Is the Ideal Time to Post On Instagram?

This differs based on the day of the week, audience, and your time zone. For instance, a college students demographic will have a lot more time to spend on Instagram during the week as opposed to a business audience which will be working and not have as much time to invest in Instagram.

This is the reason you need to determine your best time to post, which we will be covering later in this chapter. Nonetheless, there are a few days during the week and weekends, which are consistent and ideal for all brands:

- 7 – 9 am – When most people head to work

- 12 – 2 pm – Lunch breaks

- 5 – 6 pm – Close of work

- 9 -11 pm – Bedtime scrolling

As stated by research done by ShareThis, most users tend to visit Instagram during their daily commute to work. Other peak periods for Instagram activities, also include lunch break and after work hours ("The Best Time to Post on Instagram By Day, Niche & More", 2019).

Average Ideal Time to Post During the Weekend (Saturday and Sunday)

- 9 – 11 am

- 2 – 5 pm

Weekend hangovers and brunches imply that users usually pick up their phones later in the morning. Another period of high engagement is during the mid-afternoon. Since weekends are typically work-free days, the ideal time to post differs based on your audience. Note that lots of individuals go out to have fun on Saturday nights, and so depending on your target market, it may be best not to make posts late Saturday nights. According to research by HubSpot, Instagram engagement on Sunday is not great either, so it's best not to include it in your posting schedule (Chi, 2019).

Why Are These the Best Times to Post?

If you put your schedule into consideration, you will observe that your routine does not stay the same each day. These changes can have an impact on how and when you head onto social media channels.

Lots of active users on social media, go through their phones when they get up during a work week. Monday mornings are usually more tedious, so posting early Tuesday morning through Friday has tends to generate more engagement.

Also, many individuals find lunch hours to be a suitable time to head to social media. The afternoon is another period with a peak level of engagement because the mental energy of many individuals begins to wear off during this period, and social networking can offer them the much-needed break.

Saturday mornings are also peak periods that have tons of traffic on Instagram. Regardless of the activities, they are engaged in, these early hours during the weekend draw in a tremendous amount of traffic to the platform, which ensures people tend to view your content.

Determine Your Best Posting Time by Studying Your Industry Trend

Even though these general times for posting are great, to begin with, it is vital to determine your brand strategy, to enable you to target your precise audience with content relevant to them.

Sectors like tourism, technology, education, entertainment, and healthcare, do not have the same peak times. If your goal is to get to your target audience in your sector, you need to search for significant data to help you make the appropriate decisions. In doing so, you can determine the ideal time to upload your posts on Instagram.

How Does Instagram Algorithm Impact your views?

When pondering on the best posting time for Instagram, you need to learn how Instagram's algorithm has an impact on what users see. It emphasizes on recent posts, so newly uploaded posts have a higher tendency of showing up on the feeds of your users.

This algorithm influences when and if your target users will come across your posts. What this means is that you should endeavor to make your posts recent at the time your audience tends to visit Instagram.

The Instagram algorithm also analyses how much engagement a post gets when deliberating on whether to show it to your audience or not. The higher the comments, likes, and shares, the more Instagram will let your posts show up in the feeds of your audience. If you can post during peak hours, you will encourage engagement and aid each post in getting to much more of your audience.

Are Time Zones Vital?

If your core audience is situated in a precise area, like the East Coast, be certain to utilize the recommended times of their time zone. The same applies if your audience is made up of individuals who do not reside in the United States. You need to consider their time zone. You can still use the guide above even if your followers have numerous time zones.

For instance, you could upload your post to Instagram at the typical time for waking up, plan another post for mid-day, and schedule an additional post for late in the afternoon for the time zone you are targeting. If your audience is spread within numerous time zone, you can let some posts perform dual roles at once. This means they can be as a commute post in a specific time zone and after work post in another.

This may seem a little complex, but there is a range of tools that can help you with this. Instagram comes with in-built tools that can be of help, while third-party applications like Later are also at your disposal.

How to Determine the Peak Periods of Your Audience?

If your Instagram account is for business, you can take advantage of the Instagram insights tool to examine the demographics of your followers, activity, and engagement trends. This very efficient tool for analytics can aid you in making informed decisions regarding the most appropriate time for your specific audience.

You can find the data of your custom-made Instagram insights by heading to your account page via your Instagram application. Close to the top of your screen, you will find a bar graph icon –hit this, and you will find important data about how individual stories and posts are performing. You will also learn about comments, impressions, and the number of individuals that have followed and unfollowed you. With these insights, you will be able to learn the kind of content that reverberates with your audience. You will also be able to evaluate how successful your campaigns have been.

Additionally, the Followers area of Instagram insights offers you vital data about the most active period of your audience on the platform. You will be able to access a graph that lets you see the period of each day the individuals who follow you are most active and an additional graph that shows the days your followers come online. With this information, you will be able to determine activity patterns for your core audiences. Having knowledge of the times and days of peak usage will help your efforts in targeted posting.

It is vital for you to closely monitor your Instagram insight trends. However, the peak activity times of your audience will most likely change as they grow, so you need to adjust when you observe a change in the peak engagement periods. You don't want to miss the chance to connect with your audience as it develops and goes through change.

How Frequently Should You Post on Instagram?

Making frequent posts is vital to growing your following and ensuring your content gets on the feed of your audience. If you want your Instagram feed to continue being engaging and lively, you can get inspiration from established brands. According to research, leading companies upload Instagram contents 1.5 times on average each day.

How can you tap from this? Strive to upload posts one to two times each day. And the instant you have determined a posting rhythm, it is vital that you remain consistent. Imagine the effect on your account, if you made a post daily for many weeks, then reduce it suddenly to one or three times each week. Your audience may not have as much interest, and you may experience a reduction in your engagement.

To avoid this issue, it is ideal for you to begin at a slower speed. If you can manage two times a week for a start, go from there and make plans to develop with time. Ensure your focus is on quality and not quantity.

You will get a higher level of engagement by uploading amazing photos accompanied by great captions, in contrast to filling your account with substandard content.

As you understand your scheduling tool and get more comfortable with looking for content and creating it, you can increase your post frequency. The instant you have developed a regular rhythm of amazing content; your audience will be glad when you start to post more frequently.

Scheduling Posts: Why Is It Essential?

To maintain engagement and relevance on Instagram, you have to put in a lot of effort and some investigation. However, it is not compulsory to stay behind your account all day, to get to your audience. Rather, you can take advantage of scheduling tools like Later and Hootsuite.

A majority of these tools for scheduling are easy to use. And although some of them emphasize solely on scheduling, others come with in-built features for analyzing the audience. With these features, you will be able to get more insight into the engagement and activity of your audience. You will also get suggestions for the ideal posting periods tailored to your precise audience.

This can reduce the amount of manual analysis you will have to carry out, letting you pay attention to developing content of high quality with a great audience appeal. It will also inform you of the ideal time to upload posts on Instagram to ensure you satisfy your followers.

When you schedule your posts on Instagram, you will have the capacity to make your marketing efforts more efficient. Rather than posting every day, you can plan posts. Sometimes, this could be weeks or months ahead. It lets you keep an active presence on social media with much less effort. Additionally, if you develop great content, you can plan them to fall at peak periods for the broadest viewership possible.

Another benefit if using schedule tools is how you can repurpose content with ease. You will have the capacity to take a post that thrived on Instagram and share it other platforms like YouTube, LinkedIn, Facebook, and others. Better still, you can develop multi-layered campaigns, which can encourage your audience to perform a specific action, like signing up for your newsletter and attending webinars.

Understanding the ideal time to make posts on Instagram can help you generate real buyers. It is also a way of developing a successful Instagram presence. You can utilize this knowledge to offer content to the appropriate followers when the time is right, and before you know it, your follower base will grow even more.

Chapter 7
Ways to Make Money On Instagram

Instagram is a platform for sharing your passion using short videos and pictures. It also allows you to connect with individuals who share similar interests with you, develop loyal followers, and become a top influencer in your specified niche. Now, lots of accounts on Instagram have tons of followers.

Typically, many brands have noticed the room for advertising the influence and reach of these accounts can create. For this reason, users with a decent amount of followers now have numerous ways to make money using the platform. That being said, this chapter will cover the various methods you can use in earning money on Instagram. But before we delve into that, let's take a look at some of the essential things that have to be in place.

What Do You Need to Earn Cash Via Instagram?

The leverage of an Instagram user stems from the numbers of followers he/she has. The reason is that Instagram profiles that have numerous followers offer connection to a massive market. If you are serious about earning money on Instagram, you need to begin small and take all the chances possible to enhance the follower count on your account. Now, let's go into this a little further.

Influence and Reach

The natural growth of your followers has a direct relationship with the level of reach your posts have. You have numerous options to expand your posts reach, but one that is important for making cash off Instagram are authentic and original posts. You will need to have no less than three thousand followers on your profile before it becomes lucrative. This means you need to invest the time to amass followers who find you trustworthy, and who believe your posts have something significant to offer them.

If you aim to use your Instagram profile in promoting the products and services of organizations, then you need more than good reach. This is because people still have to make a move and buy the product or service you are promoting. The capacity to coax your followers into purchasing the products or services you are providing is known as influence, and if you plan on becoming a leading influencer on Instagram, you have to learn the skill of persuasion.

Even if your Instagram follower count is not a hundred thousand, there may be organizations who will be intrigued by your profile and would be keen on offering you a sponsorship if your social media presence is powerful enough to induce others to take the desired action. The level of communication you have with your followers is also as vital as your influence. If your followers don't interact with your posts, they will hardly take action.

Engaged Followers

If you are not getting comments or likes from those who follow your page, then it means your posts are not significant enough to keep them engaged and trigger a response from them. In contrast to this, if your posts are drawing in lots of likes and comments, it means the posts are helping your Instagram followers solve a specific issue they may be facing.

Also, the number of messages your Instagram followers send to you is something you should consider in determining how engaged your followers are with your posts and pages. For this reason, it is crucial that you have people continuously leaving comments on your posts, sharing them, liking them, and tagging their followers in your posts, if you are serious about sparking interest in profiles and brands that can help you make money on Instagram.

Like we covered earlier, if your posts are unable to trigger any form of response from your followers, then the number of followers won't matter. This is why you have to search for ways to enhance the number of comments and likes you get on your posts if you aim to make money on Instagram.

Now that you understand the necessary requirements, let us move on to the best ways to make money via Instagram.

Ways to Earn Money on Instagram

There are numerous ways of earning cash available at your disposal. Below are a few of the top options:

Become an Influencer

Like we have covered above, being an influencer means you can influence your followers, and control the way they feel about products and trends. This will be due to your position and the trust you have developed with your online image.

You can choose to partner with organizations as an influencer, to promote the services and products they offer. Lots of brands are eager to work with influencers to advertise their services and products. This is typically done via sponsored posts because of the numerous benefits of advertising on Instagram offers.

A sponsored post is one which displays a brand, service, or product which comes alongside branded hashtags, captions and URLs for whatever is being advertised. As an influencer, you can earn cash if you share these sponsored posts. Many companies are investing a lot of money in online advertising campaigns, and a decent portion goes to the leading influencers for every sponsored post published on their Instagram pages.

To do this effectively, you have to pick a niche that aligns with your image and lifestyle, have a specific audience, and develop authentic and relevant content. Many sponsors may even make the first contact with you if you have a decent number of followers. If you are having issues locating sponsors, there are numerous communities online you can become a member of to ensure it is less challenging to identify sponsors. A few of these include *iFluenze*, *Heartbeat*, and *TapInfluence*, among a host of others.

Use Instagram to Sell Your Photos

Instagram's core focus is on visual content. For this reason, authentic photos of high quality will help you draw in numerous buyers. These consist of pictures, videos, simple art drawings, selfies, painting, and other kinds of visual content.

If you joined Instagram because of your skill in taking photographs, there are numerous platforms where you can sell your stock pictures. You can also advertise your photos and images on Instagram using marketplaces like *Foap Community*, and *Twenty20*, among others.

In essence, if you enjoy taking pictures, this is a fantastic way of selling your work and earning cash via Instagram. Upload your images and add hashtags, captions, a personalized watermark to prevent against theft, and include the photo details to draw in prospective buyers. Take a look around the marketplace to determine the most suitable method for you.

Selling pictures is not limited to experienced photographers alone, as if you can study how to use various editing tools to create professional images; you might have a gold mine on your hands.

Become an Affiliate Marketer

Affiliate marketing shares some similarities with influencer marketing, but then there is a major difference; affiliate marketers lay emphasis on making actual sales for a commission on every sale as opposed to Influencers that help in creating awareness about a brand or product. This means if you choose to become an affiliate marketer, you are offered a commission for each product you sell.

Being an affiliate is very simple. First, you get a unique URL, which is utilized by the affiliate program in tracking the number of individuals who click on the link and make a purchase from the website. This is the way you attain your commission. These promo codes or links take users directly to the page for purchasing the product. However, Instagram does not support the placing of clickable links in any location apart from your bio, which makes it challenging to use links. For this reason, Promo codes are the best routes for affiliates as you can integrate them into your Instagram stories and posts. With this, prospective customers will only have to input your promo code when they are about checking out, for you to attain your commission, while a discount is also offered to the customer on the product.

The Unique links for promoting affiliate offers are usually quite lengthy, so you may want to use a URL Shortener to make it shorter and more customer friendly. There are numerous affiliate programs you could sign up for to begin. You can check out the range of online communities to locate the ideal affiliate program for you. Some of these communities include ***Amazon's Affiliate Program***, and ***ClickBank*** among a host of others.

Trade Your Instagram Account

Many individuals deal in exchanging Instagram accounts for funds. This may be because they no longer have an interest in using Instagram for that moment, or they have a lot of accounts with decent follower counts and are interested in making cash.

Platforms like ***Viral Accounts*** and ***Fame Swap*** are popular places to sell your Instagram accounts. Depending on the platform you choose to go with, the rates may differ, and you can do your research to find the price suitable for you and dispose of your account for a reasonable sum of cash. However, you need to think critically about this, because you never can tell when your account may be of use to you later. Before you sell-off, your account, make sure your mind has been made up.

Sell Products on Instagram

It is possible to use your Instagram profile to sell products, be it an online service, or a digital or physical product. If you have good reach on your account and you have developed awareness for the product, all that is left is for you to promote your company and watch people troop in to buy your goods or services.

Instagram has offered a very budget-friendly and easy means to buy and sell, and using this factor is quite easy. All you need to do is establish a great brand name, and when you have developed a specific level of trust, people may even begin to do your marketing for you.

A lot of entrepreneurs began their businesses from Instagram, and many of them are at the top of their fields and enjoying a continuous influx of revenue. The great news is that; there is enough space for everyone to benefit from this as well. So if you have a product to sell, Instagram may be an excellent platform to start.

Get More Website Traffic Using Instagram

If you run a business which has a website, Instagram can offer a great platform to market that business. Raise awareness for your business and upload amazing images and content that can provide your business a distinct identity, then utilize than in drawing in visitors to your site.

If your audience finds your content engaging and relevant, they will want to learn more about your organization. To make this work, you need to add a link to your website on your bio, and visitors will be directed to your website from there. In turn, this will aid in increasing your product and service awareness, and with time, your conversion.

Another excellent method of staying on top of this is to provide offers and discounts, because using exclusive offers to market your services aside from boosting your conversion, also does the same to your number of followers. This is because they will be able to locate offers that are not available in other locations. The implication of all of these is the complete growth of your business, but ensure you add a link to your website, as without it, you won't get the traffic that will help increase sales.

Drop shipping to Users on Instagram

As a drop shipper, it means you run a business without the need for a physical store. All you require is a dealer who can convey your merchandise straight from their storeroom to your clients, which eradicates having to hold expensive product inventory. You also don't have to deal with the process of shipping, and you function as your own agent.

The concept is similar to selling products; however, in this situation, you don't have to store any product of goods, which makes it seamless for entrepreneurs and owners of businesses.

There are numerous e-commerce channels like the well-recognized ones like *__Oberlo__* and *__Shopify__*, which allow you to start a drop shipping store. To begin, you have to spot an ideal niche, then try out the product market to help you determine what would sell better. If you are looking for a cheap way of becoming a business owner, then drop shipping is a fantastic option, as it doesn't require a massive sum of cash to begin selling. If you use drop shipping the right way on Instagram, there is a possibility of earning a lot of money in the long run.

With Instagram, you are open to a broad avenue of potential e-commerce. You can take advantage of the large number of individuals that are presently making money using this platform. Making money on Instagram is utterly dependent on the techniques and strategies you utilize, and the great thing is that you can invest yourself in more than one channel and be successful in them all. Now, all that is left is for you to head out and earn money via the Instagram platform. However, even if you understand how to make money on Instagram, if you don't know how to promote your services or the products you sell, nobody may even approach you in the first place. The next chapter will be digging into how you can exploit Instagram ads.

Chapter 8
Taking Advantage of Instagram Ads

Instagram gets over one billion visitors each month. In addition to this, the numbers of engagement for this application is way more than Twitter and Facebook combined. This means you are losing out big time if you are not taking advantage of what the app has to offer.

This is the reason why this chapter will be teaching you how Instagram advertising works, and all the vital information regarding Instagram ads, so you can get your content across to the individuals on Instagram who matter to you. But first, we will be looking into what Instagram ad is.

Instagram Ads – What Is It?

Limited ad services were first introduced by Instagram when Facebook took over ownership in 2013. However, it only began to provide advertising access to various sizes of businesses and brands in 2015. These brands soon realized that Instagram was of enormous benefit for businesses.

Also, because Instagram is incorporated with Facebook Ads Manager, brands can take advantage of the enormous resources of user data Facebook offers, to advertise right to the audience they desire.

If you prefer numbers to understand how beneficial Instagram ads can be, below are a few statistics;

- Seventy-five percent of the Instagram users perform an action via Instagram ads like heading to a site or buying a product.

- Thirty-five percent of adults in America utilize Instagram("22+ Instagram Statistics That Matter to Marketers in 2019", 2019).

In essence, if you are not taking advantage of Instagram ads, you are depriving yourself of a considerable amount of possible revenue.

What Is the Cost of Instagram Ads?

Depending on your ad objectives, the cost may be unique to you. This is because all ads differ. However, for Instagram ads, the typical CPC (cost-per-click) is about $0.70 — $0.80. This figure was obtained from an evaluation of over $300million spent on ads. ("Instagram Ad Costs: The Complete Updated Resource for 2018", 2018)

Note that this is just like an estimate. You may end up spending more or less depending on numerous factors like the time of the year ads are set-up.

Creating Ads on Instagram

Now that you understand the basics, we will be taking a look at how to create ads. For this, we will be learning to do it using the Facebook Ad Manager, which is a prevalent method because it is easy to use. It also offers you the capacity to personalize your ad more than you would if you were using the application itself. Below are the steps that can help you create your ad.

Head to the Ad Manager via Facebook

Presuming you already have a Facebook account, and you are logged in, all you need to do is follow this link to get to the Facebook ad manager.

There is no precise Instagram Ad manager. You oversee Instagram ads via the Facebook Ads UI.

Determine Your Marketing Goals

Here, you need to pick a campaign goal. The great news is that the goals are clearly stated. If you are after additional traffic, select the traffic goal. If you want more engagement, choose the engagement goal, and so on.

However, there are only a few goals you can work with using Instagram ads, which include;

- Traffic

- Brand awareness

- Video Views

- Engagement: which works for just post engagement

- Conversions

- Reach

- App Installs

Determine your Target Audience

After determining your objective, you have to target the right audience, so your ad gets to the appropriate individuals. This is where Instagram ads flourish since you will be utilizing the demographic knowledge Facebook offers to get to the right individuals.

If you have previously utilized Facebook ads, you may have already built some audiences and understand the entire process. If you are using it for the first time, below are the targeting options you have at your disposal, which you can narrow down to reach a specific audience. For example, if you want to target men in Chicago, between the ages of 18- 25, who have an interest in sporting equipment, you will have the capacity to do that.

The targeting actions include;

- **Location**: lets you target a city, state, country, or zip code and ignore specific areas.

- **Gender**: Pick between all genders, or only men and vice versa

- **Age**: Lets you target different age ranges

- **Demographics**: You can access this under Detailed Targeting. It also has numerous sub-categories to pick from.

- **Languages**: Facebook suggests that you leave this place blank unless the language you want to target is not typical in the area you are aiming to target.

- **Behaviors**: This is also an option you will find under Detailed Targeting. It also provides you with numerous categories to check out. It could either be anniversaries, purchasing behaviors, job roles, and a host of other options.

- **Interests**: Still another option you will have access to under Detailed Targeting which offers numerous sub-categories to delve into. If you are in search of individuals who have an interest in horror movies, or beverages, you get these options and many more.

- **Custom Audience**: With this option, you will be able to upload your contact list and target leads or clients who you aim to upsell.

- **Lookalike Audience**: Here, Instagram gives you the chance to locate audiences who share lots of similarities to your other audiences.

- **Connections**: Here, you can target individuals connected to your app, page, or event.

After configuring your audience, Facebook also offers you a guide to how broad or specific your audience is. It is vital you take note of this because you want to choose a point where your audience is not too broad since it is not adequately targeted, but you don't want it to be too narrow either, since you may be unable to reach that many individuals.

Determine your Placements

The next step after targeting the demographic of your choice is to select your placement. This is vital if your campaign objectives are to show the ads on Instagram alone. If you decide to forgo this step, Facebook will let your ads show up on the two platforms.

This can be a positive thing, but if you have created content for Instagram, specifically, you need to pick the option "Edit Placements." From this point, you can choose Instagram as your placement, and if you would prefer the ads to show up on the stories or feed area of the platform. You also have the option of letting it show up on both.

Determine your Ad Schedule and Budget

If you understand how budgets work via AdWords, Facebook, and other platforms for running an ad, you may not have many issues with this step. If you have not, then it is not so much of a problem either, even though you may not understand how to put your lifetime or daily budget in place while running an Instagram campaign for the first time, you learn on the go. What's more, you also can pause or stop your ad at any point, if you believe your budget is not being apportioned the right way.

So which should you go with? A daily or lifetime budget? This is solely dependent on you, but if you decide to go with a daily budget, it ensures your budget does not get exhausted fast. In contrast, a lifetime budget gives you the capacity for scheduling your ad delivery. Both options do the work they should, so it is a matter of choice.

As mentioned earlier, you can schedule an ad to target certain moments of the week or day, that experience peak activity from your audience. If you are utilizing a lifetime budget, this can be an essential way of optimizing your budget.

Develop Your Instagram Ad

Here comes the moment you need to create your ad. Here, the set-up may seem different based on the objective you decide to go with.

There are six ad formats which Instagram provides you with. From the options provided, two show up on Instagram stories, while the other four show up on your Instagram feed. The latter is the option many marketers and advertisers take advantage of.

The options available include;

- Image Feed Ads

- Image Story Ads

- Video Feed Ads

- Video Story Ads

- Carousel Feed Ads

- Canvas Story ads

Every one of these ad formats is incorporated into the Stories and Feeds of the users which offer a non-distracting experience for users. Instagram also provides you a range of call-to-actions which can aid you in attaining more leads. We will be taking a look at each of them below:

Image Feed Ads

This is the most common ad format, and if you frequently use Instagram, there is a huge possibility that you may have come across it while perusing your feed. These ads consist of a single image which shows up when your target audience is going through their feed. The great thing about this ad is that if you do them properly, they will look like any other feed instead of ads.

Some of the specifications for this ad include:

- Type of file: Jpeg or PNG

- Max size of the file: 30MB

- Number of Hashtags: Maximum of 30

- Length of Text: 2,200 max. However, for the best delivery, Instagram suggests you stay below 90 characters.

Image Story Ads

This is similar to the Image feed ads, but they show up on the Instagram Stories of your target.

The specifications include:

- 9:16 recommended image ratio and no less than 600 pixels' image width.

Video Feed Ads

You can give your ad more life using a video. If you create a video of high quality, then it is possible to promote it via your Instagram feed. Instagram offers support for various video files, but it is suggested that you use: square pixels, progressive scan, fixed frame rate, H.264 compression, and a 128kbps+ stereo AAC audio compression.

However, if you do have a video which fails to meet these requirements, numerous apps can aid you in altering your video.

Some of the specifications for video feed ads include:

- video resolution: No less than 1080 x 1080 pixels'

- Max file size: 4GB

- Max length of video: 60 seconds

- 125 characters' text length recommended

- Number of Hashtags: Maximum of 30

Video Story Ads

Stories are also great locations for running ads. This is because lots of users often expect to see videos here so it may not come as a surprise to see ads. The specifications for these ads are listed below:

- Video Resolution: No less than 1080 x 1920 pixels

- Video Length: Maximum of 15 seconds

- Maximum file size: 4GB

Carousel Feed Ads

Depending on how you use it, this format of ads can be quite fun. It lets you display a group of images users can scroll through instead of just one image. This kind of ad is ideal for brands that are very visual like those in the clothing industry, travel industry, food industry, and vehicle industry, among others.

You can use this to show your audience the faces behind your organization. The carousel feed ads let you include as much as ten images in one ad, all with a link to each product. Also, you have the option of adding a video to this form of ad.

The specifications for this ad include:

- Type of file: JPG or PNG

- Number of Hashtags: Maximum of 30

- Length of Text: 2,200 max. However, for the best delivery, Instagram suggests you stay below 90 characters.

- Max file size: 30MB

- Length of Video: Maximum of 60 seconds

Canvas Story Ads

Finally, the most recent inclusion to the ad formats, Canvas ads. With these ads, you can create a VR experience in your story. They only function on mobile devices and give you complete control of customization options. However, you need some technical knowledge. These ads can work alongside video, image, and carousel.

The specifications for this format are:

- Minimum width of the image: 400 pixels

- Max Height of Image: 150 pixels

Determining the Best Ad Format to Use On Instagram

Having understood the formats, you can choose from; you need to determine the best format for your needs.

You need to be deliberate about your ad format, and the question below can help you make a choice:

What Is Your Objective?

Your desired social media objective is the foundation for all the conclusions you make when it has to do with an ad campaign. It will aid you in determining what you should focus on and what you should not.

Any ad you choose has to align with your objectives, always remember that.

Tips for Advertising On Instagram

Now that you understand the technical aspects of ad creation, below are a few things to note when developing an ad that will ensure engagement;

Know Your Audience

When you have an in-depth knowledge of your audience, you will be able to create messaging that they can connect with.

Before you begin to run any ads, you must have an intimate and in-depth knowledge of your audience.

Ask yourself:

- What solution does your service or product provide to them?

- What are their wants and needs?

- Do not forget their values and goals as you put your ads in place.

Utilize Texts Properly

Instagram does not let you use too many texts, but it does not have to be a negative thing. However, this means you need to offer the best value within the supported text character. While using your texts, ensure you are considering the personas of your audience.

Put engaging and appealing CTAs in place that will encourage your audience to perform any action you require.

Take Advantage of Hashtags

Many individuals tend to forget just how powerful hashtags can be. But if you learn to use them the right way, you will have an indispensable tool in your hands.

Including hashtags in Instagram posts enhances engagement by an average of 12.6 percent, which can make a whole lot of difference to your campaign. And if you take advantage of a branded hashtag, it can enhance awareness and engagement.

You have the capacity of utilizing as much as 30 hashtags on a single post. But don't get carried away; focus on the quality as opposed to the quantity.

Engage

You can group the interaction you have with social media users into two classes:

- Reactive Interaction: when you provide responses to mentions, direct messages, and comments on social media.

- Proactive Interaction: When you make the first contact with other users by engaging them. This can be very beneficial if you want to enhance the awareness around specific product launches or campaigns.

Ensure you do a bit of both as people engage and respond to your ads. It will help in developing your brand and ensure they understand you are not just another robotic organization.

82

Stay Consistent

Are you aware that more than 50 percent of the leading brands utilize a similar filter for each of their posts? ("33 Mind-Boggling Instagram Stats & Facts for 2018", 2019) The reason for this is simple: Consistency can aid in strengthening the image of your brand.

Every component of your brand should embody who you are as an organization. The tone, message, and visuals are all vital.

Regularly Switch Things Up

When you create a good ad, which seems to be doing so well and bringing you lots of engagement and traffic, it is easy to get attached. However, a great ad can only last for so long and may die down if you keep rinsing and repeating.

Change your ads as frequently as possible, so your audience doesn't get fed up with them. In addition to this, it will also help you understand the ads that offer you the best results. Try using various formats, captions, and audiences.

Measure Ad Performance

Using the Facebook Ads Manager, you can check out how your Instagram ads are performing. If you are using third party tools like Hootsuite Ads, you will be provided with a more comprehensive set of data that lets you view the best performing ads and those that are not working —and why they aren't.

In any strategy, monitoring performance and altering course when needed is very vital. But you also need to regularly check your Instagram analytics for a range of reasons which include:

- It can help you put in place realistic objectives and goals for every new campaign.

- It can help you monitor your competitors

Try Out Your Ad Copy

You need to try out various ad visuals and copy in a single campaign as it will also help things remain fresh.

Chapter 9
Targeting and Retargeting On Instagram

As a marketer, it can be quite infuriating to learn that prospective clients are slipping from your purchase funnel, for something that was not your fault. The internet offers a lot of distractions, and clients may check out your page, put a few products in their carts on your website, then they get distracted by something else and don't remember to make the final purchase.

The good news is that tracking these kinds of engagement and subtly pushing users to complete these actions is possible using Retargeting. In this chapter, we will learn what retargeting is and how you can include it in your marketing efforts. **What is Retargeting?**

In the digital space of today, retargeting is a very efficient method of converting leads. It is also known as remarketing, and it is a technique that has to do with taking previous leads –individuals who previously checked out your website, placed an item in their shopping cart or clicked an ad, and contacting them once more in a bid to convert them to final consumers.

They are ads which are structured in the form of reminders. The aim of retargeting is to help you make sales from the various existing audiences and leads you have. Retargeting offers a lot of potential to enhance your customer base, sales, and profits. This is because only around 2 percent of the primary web traffic leads to conversion the first time(Dunn, 2019). If you channel your resources into consistent and frequent retargeting efforts across all social media platforms, your possibilities are endless. If you are still not convinced about how retargeting can help your business, check out why retargeting is essential today.

Why Should You Retarget?

There are lots of individuals who may be skeptical of retargeting because it mainly has to do with keeping track of visitors. This can bring about some worries of privacy as many people have at some point gotten creeped out by continuous ads for an item we ran a search for in a store, months back.

If you do it the right way, retargeting does not have to bother anyone. If your tone and approach are strategic and authentic, you can be offering your audience an excellent service by jogging their memories about the presence of your brand. In the end, retargeting is one of the most efficient methods of offering viewers relevant ads built around their past behaviors and interests.

Aside from subtly nudging people to complete a purchase, you will also have the capacity to target your website visitors who checked out your tutorials or pricing pages. It will let you provide ads that directly satisfy their needs or interests. Also, with the growth of social media platforms which are driven by interest like Facebook, users have become familiar with the existence of interest-target ads, which makes remarketing something to expect.

Even though cookies and various tracking mechanisms have been around for a while, the process has been made easier for organizations to access due to the advent of Facebook's Pixel. When you incorporate Facebook Pixel to your site, you will have the capacity to participate in conversion tracking and build audiences based on views of a specific webpage.

Remarketing on a platform like Instagram, which many organizations and brands have not fully explored, can provide you with the capacity to locate new audiences on this incredibly visual platform. Furthermore, the integration of Facebook ads with Instagram also ensures it is less difficult to employ remarketing ads, which lead to high levels of conversions, thereby offering you more profit and a broader audience base. Now that you know why retargeting is something to take advantage of let's find out the steps to take for retargeting on Instagram.

Steps for Retargeting On Instagram

To accurately retarget on Instagram, the steps below can ensure you are successful

Install Facebook Pixel

The first thing you need to do is install the Facebook Pixel on your site. Pixel is an excellent tool for retargeting efforts. It is solely devoted to keeping track of all individuals that check out your website. With the data it offers, you will have a continuously increasing list of users, who are sure to know your product to some extent. If you don't know how to go about installing Facebook pixel on your site, you can offer the code to your site developer so they can get it done for you.

To ensure the pixel has been adequately integrated on your website, use the FB Pixel Helper, which is a plugin tool for Google Chrome, to find out.

Create The Audience You Want to Retarget

Next, you need to put a custom audience in place. These are the individuals you plan to send your ads to. Facebook gives you the chance to pick Website Traffic as the set of individuals to send ads to. This lets you draw in users who opened your website from the Custom Audience Pixel you have installed and lets them see your ads one more time.

To build your custom audience of individuals who have checked out your site in the past few days, all you have to do is head to your Facebook ads manager, then you select Tools – Audiences – Create Audience – Custom Audience – Website Customization. Then, pick your customization. When creating your audience, its best to choose those who visited your website during the past 180 days, as that is the highest option available.

Develop your Ad Campaign

Before you take this step, you have to hold on until people pay a visit to your website for the pixel to increase. See it this way; every visitor to your site with an account on Facebook is being lodged in a guest house, and when the guest house has enough lodgers, you can create your ad and target every individual in that guest house.

Depending on the level of traffic you get to your website, this may require only some minutes to a week. When you have adequate individuals in your audience, you will see "Ready" alongside a green dot.

If you have a reasonable amount of individuals in your "Retargeting Audience," you can then develop your ad campaign. To do this, create your Instagram ad campaign following the usual steps like we covered in Chapter 8.

Create Your Retargeting Ad Set

Here, you will determine the campaign's Ad set level. To start, set the schedule and designed budget you want the ad to run from. Next, pick the Custom Audience you created in the second step and set the ad's

88

placement as Instagram. Next, make sure that there are individuals in your Audience by making sure your potential reach is more than 20.

If you are working with the typical Ads Manager, ensure only Instagram is selected and every other option is deselected if you want to use it for placement.

Create Your Retargeting Ad

Now you can create an ad that will be seen physically by your audience. Do not forget that people who have visited your website previously and have knowledge of who you are and what you do are categorized as "warm traffic" so you need to add some creativity to your ads.

Pick the appropriate Instagram and Facebook accounts and include the destination. Next, create an enticing ad that will lure your "warm traffic" to head back to your site and make a purchase or perform any other action you desire. If you want a more direct option for retargeting, try the Instagram dynamic ads.

Use Instagram Dynamic Ads for Targeting and Retargeting

Instagram Dynamic Ads was launched in 2016. It aids in advertising your products by letting people see ads that consist of products they previously showed an interest in –either by including it to their shopping carts or viewing it. The products shown to them could also be similar to what they purchased or displayed interest in.

On Facebook, more than 2 billion distinct items and products have been uploaded. Now, with Dynamic Ads being offered on Instagram, you can promote relevant merchandise to users who have checked your website across Instagram and Facebook.

This is the way to go if you want a straightforward method. You can automatically retarget the right individuals by showing them products they previously checked out. This is just another way for you to retarget via Instagram.

Takeaway

A poor retargeting strategy can be annoying from the client's perspective. This is the case where they continuously have to deal with ads from web pages they have no interest in.

However, Instagram comes in a design that gives your brand the chance to connect with audiences in a manner which is visual and not as intrusive as other platforms. There are retargeting campaigns that are properly created and targeted that viewers don't see as adverts but important reminders that direct them to make a purchase. This is the case with Airbnb's retargeting campaign.

When it comes to marketing on social media, regardless of the platform, the best strategy is to accept testing and repetition. Even if your brand has no plans to create a full-time campaign on Instagram, you can take advantage of the Facebook Pixel and get vital information to help you target the right users. Now is the time to retarget, with Facebook Pixel and its capacity to work on two of the leading platforms: Instagram and Facebook, it has never been any easier. Retargeting is a way of ensuring those who got to your page, buy your product. But how do you use Instagram to transform them into loyal customers in the first place? The next chapter will help you unravel this.

Chapter 10
How to Turn Your Audience Into Customers

As a marketer or business owner, it is not entirely difficult to get new followers or audience. All you need to do as we have covered in earlier chapters is to stay consistent and share valuable content. However, when it comes to transforming the audience into paying customers, it is another story entirely, and you need to do more than post each day.

As stated by studies, 71% of individuals have a higher likelihood to purchase a product via recommendations from social media, while 74% get directions from social media when making purchase decisions ("How To Make An Impact On Consumers Mind | Lemonz Studios", 2018). What this means is that, when it comes to making decisions related to a purchase, customers are more devoted to social media.

As someone who provides or advertises products and services, it will only be to your benefit if you leverage this trend. Now, Instagram is the fastest rising social platform. In addition to being attractive and user-friendly to the younger generations, it also offers a barrage of benefits that can help your business make more sales. For this reason, you need to take all the necessary steps to transform your audience to life-long customers. This is what this chapter will elaborate on as we will be covering some techniques that can help you with this below.

Turning Your Audience into Customers

Below are a few tips that can help you transform your audience to life-long customers.

Do Some Research

As you begin to notice an increase in your followers count, take some time to learn what they have an interest in and who they are. What do they like? Are they professionals or students? Do they have a pending need? Are they your ideal clients?

Determining these is vital for a few reasons. First, when you know your followers, you can make your connection more personalized. Leave a comment on one of their posts. Doing this may not take more than a minute, but the effect to your customer can be of very high value.

Next, if you don't have an image of your perfect customer yet, it will help you start creating one. But, if you already have a clear picture, you can keep track of how properly you are drawing them in and help them meet their needs.

Provide Special Content

By providing exclusive content to your audience, you can further enhance the relationship you share with them. This will ensure they keep returning to you continuously and urges them to engage with your business on a personal level, and a long term basis.

The following are ways you can do this:

- Provide exclusive footage: Utilize Instagram to disclose products you have not shared on other platforms like Twitter or Facebook. Doing this will make your followers on Instagram feel special.

- Develop an exclusive offer: Provide a discount code to your Instagram followers, which you are letting them have.

- Launch an event or product via Instagram: Create a brief video of your organization taking a trip, or opening a new outlet.

Leverage Promotion

Promote a part of your business by establishing a social media giveaway which your fans will find exciting. This is vital because it helps your followers understand what you offer and what you do. It also helps in generating more engagement on your various pages on social media.

For instance, you can ask: "What is your best budgeting tip? The first respondent will be offered a free meeting with me on how to create a proper budget."

Structure Your Business or Store to Seem Amazing

One of the leading techniques you can use in transforming your audience into customers on Instagram is to create a business profile people would want to associate themselves with.

To do this, display pictures of your business place being a fun place to be. Imagine an image showing your co-workers having a team bonding weekend at the beach or a weekend barbecue. There are lots of ways you can spin this. Feel free to be creative here.

Another way to ensure your followers are more involved in your brand or company is to provide them with exclusive behind the scenes footage into the task you are working on.

A few ways to do this include:

- Show a picture of a product being sent to a customer

- Post an image of a meeting where your co-workers are busy speaking about a product.

- Show the before or after image of a meeting.

Be Loyal

To get loyal customers, you need to have loyal followers and fans. But if you want loyalty, you have to give allegiance.

And how is the best way to do this?

It is by staying consistent. Showing respect, care, and consistency will help in showing loyalty. To do this effectively, consistently post content –regardless of if you need to publish at particular weekdays or you upload a few posts each day. Pick one and stick to it, so your followers will know when your posts will come in.

If you need to go on a break, that is not a problem, but ensure you let your followers know about it. For instance, if you are going on a trip, inform them beforehand and tell them you can't wait to be back. You can also let them be aware that you may not keep to schedule during your absence. Doing this proves that you respect the connection with them and their time.

Similarly, to show care and concern, prove to them that their opinions are significant. If they leave comments, do not ignore them. Prove that you care about them each day, similarly as you do about your friends around you.

Invite them to A Personalized and Entertaining Event

You should learn to treat your followers like royalty. People are most likely to purchase from brands that give them the best treatment. For example, you can invite your Instagram followers to a live session where you will provide responses to their questions in your area of experience.

Let them know that you will be responding to questions from the first 20 or 30 people as the case may be. Don't forget to inform them of the time you will be available to respond to their questions.

You can also request that followers send their questions to your DM in advance if they are unable to meet the allocated date/time. In addition to being beneficial to them, it also ensures that you can begin the event seamlessly because you don't need to hold on for someone to ask a question. Instead, the first 10 minutes can be devoted to answering questions from the DM.

Develop Exclusive Deals for your Followers

Let your followers know they are unique. By creating exclusive deals, your followers will keep coming back repeatedly. You don't need to create excessively complex deals, let them be fun and straightforward as it tends to work better.

For instance: "If you purchase a (specific) item today, you will get a 30% off – Exclusive to our Instagram followers. Send us a mail and let us know you saw this post!

Also, you can begin a deal of the week. All of these will ensure followers continue to come back and check in to see what is new. And whenever they do need a service or product you sell, you will be the first they come running to.

Promote Your Followers

Doing this is a fantastic way to gain credibility, give back, and strengthen relationships. The instant you have developed a good relationship; followers transform into customers.

Choose a specific weekday on your Instagram page to advertise a follower. You can use a hashtag of your choice like #followerappreciation and promote a follower. To effectively do this, don't include numerous followers in a single post, as this makes it random and not personal.

Instead, pick a follower that you engage with a lot and make a post about him/her letting them know why their connection is significant to you. To go further with this, you can leave the first comment explaining why you appreciate them and the value they have added to you.

Run Contests on Instagram

Contests are a great way to get leads from Instagram. Not only do people love competing against one another, but they also love free prizes.

First, you need to come up with a great theme. Most contests are successful because they correspond with something the followers have in mind already. So let your contest be centered around a specific season or holiday. Ensure you communicate the prize to be won and that it is substantial enough to urge your followers to partake in the contest. A great technique is to pick a prize that your target market will find appealing.

To take things further, you can add an element of voting. This could be in the lines of: "Whoever gets 500 likes wins a prize". Including this is beneficial to you because it ensures you have a higher chance of trending because of your content, which in turn provides an increase in your brand awareness. The reason is simple; people participating in the contest will inform their family and friends to turn in votes, and the friends will also inform their friends and so on. This can be a great way to get leads as someone who is in search of a service you render may just be directed to your page.

Leverage Testimonials

You are more likely to get a customer from your followers if one or more of your followers have something great to say about their experience with your business.

Take note of the good things people say about your business and request their permission to share on your page. When you share testimonials, it reminds your followers that you offer a specific product or service. Also, it lets others know that those that did business with you found your products or services to be of value.

Take Advantage of Shoppable Posts

It can be quite frustrating to hold onto a customer and get them to take the step of heading to your website and making a purchase decision. However, with the new shoppable post feature, you can now redirect your followers to your product page directly from a post. Simply put; your posts will be like a standard post, but you will have the capacity to tag products on it.

It is less complicated for your prospective clients and followers to see the product, as opposed to heading to your site on their own and searching manually for an item. With a shoppable post, you can turn your followers into customers as the posts will come with the price and link to buy a product. What is left for a customer will be to hit the tag, and they will be diverted to the page of the product.

Strike a Balance

Not many people will buy from you if all you do is continuously promote new products or redirect your followers to your website. Many people won't even stick around in the first place. The same applies to any strategy you choose. Doing the same thing continuously can become predictable and even boring after a while.

But if you continue to switch things and create a balance between promotion, and interaction, then your followers will be happy to continue the interaction later. They will always look forward to what you have to share each day.

Chapter 11
Taking Advantage of Stories and Contests on Instagram

Instagram stories like we have covered earlier, shares a lot of similarities with Snapchat. With this feature, you can share videos and images which will vanish 24hours after being uploaded. However, Instagram stories can provide an avenue for brands and marketers to get to a more significant number of people, if done the right way.

According to Instagram, stories have urged users to spend more time on the platform and pay more frequent visits. Users less than the age of 25 spend over 32 minutes daily on Instagram, while the older age groups spend over 24 minutes daily on the platform ("22+ Instagram Statistics That Matter to Marketers in 2019", 2019).

This feature offers you a few seconds to prove to millions of individuals that your service or product is worth it, so how do you do it in a way that will ensure conversions? The tips below can help you begin.

Integrate Polls in Instagram Stories

Individuals and brands now can include engaging polls to their stories. In addition to being entertaining, these polls are a great means of engaging with your audience and getting their opinions on various subjects. By taking advantage of the change to get the opinion of your audience on a decision or subject, you could help save money, energy, and time which could be channeled to other areas of your business.

On Travel Tuesday, Airbnb requested that its audience took part in a poll. As straightforward as it seemed, it was well-organized and very professional. Airbnb leveraged the content followers generated, thereby achieving two objectives simultaneously: Airbnb interacts with the content of its followers, and the job of developing a Story becomes less demanding by taking the content already in existence ("Top 10 Successful Hashtag Campaigns That Created an Impact", 2019).

Many brands and influencers have experienced a rise in stories engagement and Instagram live since they started taking advantage of the polls feature. With the help of Instagram insights, they can monitor engagement for entire feeds or per post during a specific period.

Take Advantage of Links

One of the fantastic perks of social media is the intimate relationship brands will create with their followers. Stories have given your brand the chance to take this intimacy a bit further. But, if your brand is not taking advantage of the attention stories provide, then this connection goes down the drain. The least difficult method of leveraging this attention is via direct links.

A significant aspect of Instagram Stories for business is the capacity to link and tag. Using this great feature, you are privy to link your pages. If you are a marketer, you can link product pages where your audience can make purchases immediately. When viewers of your stories swipe up, they get redirected to the page of your choice. As a marketer, you can also link forms for lead generations from any of your marketing software, to add more numbers to your email list. This feature can only be accessed by business profiles that have over 10,000 followers. If you don't meet this criterion, you can choose the option of including a short URL or place a link in your bio which may not be as effective. However, the possibilities at your disposal here are quite enormous.

Tell an Actual Story of Your Brand

The introduction of stories has proven that there is significant value in authentic content in the eyes of your audience. For this reason, when you document your journey, your brand becomes more approachable.

This means you need to use your stories to tell a real story. Tell stories concerning the services and products you provide. This can help in developing the loyalty of brands, which increases the possibility of referrals and purchase.

Perfect instances of digital storytelling include factories showing how a specific product is developed, restaurant showing how specific meals are prepared and makeup brands showing how to tutorials. You have the power to be as creative as you can while doing this.

Use Overlay Text to Magnify CTAs

Typically, you can find the CTA beneath the screen. However, it is quite little and not difficult to miss. Ensure your viewers are aware of what action you need them to take by leveraging on text overlay to recap the CTA in large and bold lettering.

When you develop your stories, ensure you pick the appropriate CTA button that you want to show up. The words you choose, the size of your letters, and the text color can have a lot of impact on if viewers check out your site, sign up or become actual leads. As a marketer, you can include active verbs like "Buy Now." However, if your goal is to generate leads, you can utilize "Sign up Today" etc.

Leverage Instagram Takeovers

Instagram takeovers are fast, fun, and easy methods for boosting your following either by taking control of another user's Instagram account or letting them take control of yours, usually for a period of 24-hours. This is a fantastic way of developing a relationship which is mutually beneficial between your brand and another influencer. Also, it offers an amazing means for growing your audience. The possibilities are limitless.

An easy way for you to do this for your brand or company is to pick a person in your organization to post stories showing how a typical day is for them. Better still, you can collaborate with other brands in the same field as you to trade stories for the day. This will aid in diversifying your content and ensure your clients keep heading back for more.

By aligning your brand with someone who has something of value to add to your desired objective, it encourages genuinely and helps you connect with followers who want to interact with your brand, which in turn makes your network broader.

Utilize Instagram Story Ads

In January 2017, Instagram kick-started the Stories ad function with brands like Airbnb, Netflix, and Nike. Later in March, this feature was opened to various sizes of organizations. When developing your ad, it is vital to quickly get the attention of your followers or audience. Photo ads only remain for 10 seconds, while video ads have a 15 seconds time frame before they vanish.

What this means is that you need to make certain that you can pass across the message effectively during the first seconds of your ad, to enable them to take a step the moment it is done. You need to keep the user interested with powerful visuals, keep them engaged with flawless messaging, and subtly nudge them into taking action.

If you decide to go with photo ads, make sure you utilize a photo which is bright and bold. It should also have simple messaging and clear branding. The user needs to be able to tell with ease who you are, what you do, and how you can assist them fast before the end of the ad. If you meet all of the conditions, your Instagram Stories can quickly go viral, and you don't want to ensure you don't exhaust your budget. To curb this, you need to be on the lookout to ensure you don't go past your daily limit.

Why You Need to Begin Using Instagram Stories Ads

Instagram Stories ads are ideal for reaching new audiences and advertising your business, brand, and products to an audience which is already engaged. Instagram Stories already has a very high rate of Engagement, with Instagram stating that one out of five stories gets a DM from viewers.

Instagram Stories ads are a vital aspect of any Instagram marketing strategy, and it gives you the chance to be as creative as you can. If you are using stories and getting a great level of engagement from them, then there is nothing stopping you from taking advantage of Instagram Stories ads as well. Instagram stories ads offer you a range of options to choose from which include:

- **Video** ads: These play for 15 seconds before they vanish. You can edit one of your own, or create on via the Ads manager or Facebook's Creative Hub.

- Photo: A motionless image ad which will last for 5 seconds. You can upload one of your designs, or create on via the Ads manager or Facebook's Creative Hub.

- Carousel: These allow you to play as much as three content pieces in a single ad. This could be photos and videos in one ad.

Now that you know what Instagram Stories ads, let's look into some few things to add in your design, and how you can kick-off your first ad campaign on Instagram Stories.

Create a Plan for Your Ad Design

You need to understand that users have the choice of skipping Instagram Stories ads, so this implies that the video and image you integrate into the ad is appealing enough to instantly draw the attention of your viewers.

In designing your ad, you can get the help of an experienced designer or advertising agency that knows how the platform works. You can also develop the ad by yourself with the help of visual design tools.

If you make the choice of using a single image to design your ad, you need to ensure you begin with a high-quality visual. Next, include straightforward but commanding text on the image. An image ad vanishes in 10 seconds, so you need to ensure the message you want to pass is clear. Let your viewers understand what your business does and how you can offer them this service.

It is recommended by Facebook that the size of your image is 1080 x 1920, with a 9:16 aspect ratio. If you would rather go with the option of videos as opposed to an image, ensure your video is in MP4, MOV or GIF format, with a length of no more than 15 seconds. The video can have a size as large as 2.3 GB with no lower than 720p resolution. Note that you will be able to use text like messages, descriptions, title, and other captions.

The instant you have a final video or image you plan on utilizing in your ad, you can now head to the process of developing your Instagram Stories campaign.

Develop Your Ad

In the development of your Instagram Stories ad, you can take advantage of either Power Editor or the Facebook Ads Manager. When you develop your ad, what you need to do first is to pick a campaign objective. Presently, the only objective you can pick for this sort of campaign is Reach. But according to Facebook, later on, there will be other objectives available like Mobile App Installs, Website Clicks, and Web Conversions, among others.

Next, provide your campaign with a name and hit Continue. The instant you are through defining your campaign audience, head to placements, and choose the option for Edit Placements. Then, pick stories under Instagram. Remember that after choosing Stories, the other placements will no longer be checked because you won't be able to run an Instagram Stories ad for any other placement.

After setting up your scheduling or budget, you can then move on to designing your ad. First, you have to select the format for your ad. You can choose to utilize a single video or single image for your ad. Once your selection has been made, the next step is to upload your video or image file. If you choose to go with a video upload, you will be provided with an option to select a preview image when you are finished with the upload.

After you are through with your media upload, you can find out if you want to enter tags or track your campaign. Then, you can now kick-off your campaign. Now, let's move on to how you can leverage contests for your brand.

How Can Brands Take Advantage of Contests?

Determining how you can kick-off a positive contest on Instagram is not as straightforward as other strategies on the platform. The great thing about contests is that they take advantage of UGC (User-generated content) and do not need as much devotion from individuals involved in it.

Lots of users are eager to jump on an offer to win a free flight to their dream destination for posting a selfie with a hashtag or uploading a specific picture. This is what makes Instagram contests appealing and one of the most effective strategies to enhance engagement and boost your audience fast. From lots of appealing freebies to free trips, there are lots of directions your Instagram contest can take.

The Benefit of Instagram Contests for Brands

Instagram is already perfectly set-up for UGC campaigns. Users are already distributing their videos and photos on Instagram. If you can look for a means by which your brand can deviate those existing habits and interest **to where you want them**, you will have the means of engaging users on Instagram in a relevant and entertaining way.

Integrating Instagram contents in your strategy for marketing can aid you in boosting your follower count, broadening your reach, and developing loyal ambassadors for your brand. In this section, we will be looking into a few things that can make your Instagram contest a success.

Plan Your Goals and Objectives

It is vital for you to make a comprehensive plan before you go to a marketing contest on Instagram. For a contest to be a success, its goal must be one that is in line with the behaviors and interests of your target audience.

Regardless of what your objectives are, it is vital that you put a precise goal in place, so you are aware of the contest was a success or not. To aid in streamlining your focus, consider the audience you want to reach. Ask yourself the following:

- What types of posts do they love to see on your account?

- What types of posts do they like to post on their feeds?

- How is their behavior on the platform?

If your goal is to increase your engagement, you should focus on building your purpose and content around content that your followers already want to interact with or post.

Remember to put a budget and time-frame in place for your contest, because deciding these details in advance will aid you in designing a more effective contest.

Put an Entry Method in Place

There are numerous ways for you to develop contests on Instagram, even though the most engaging and efficient contests on Instagram are those that urge your followers to upload photos of their own. Due to this, it is vital for you to create your guidelines and let your audience know what they require to be a part of the contest.

Below are a few concepts you can use as entry methods for your contests:

- Get your followers to upload a video or image to Instagram using a particular theme or hashtag.

- Get your audience to follow you alongside uploading a post, or get them to follow you alone.

- Get your followers to tag your brand in a post they upload.

- Get your audience to comment or like one of your posts.

Ensure you properly plan what the rules are for partaking in the contest, and try to be certain that they are explicitly stated during your promotion. Perhaps the contest has to do with a hashtag not consisting of your brand name. If you want to get recognition for your brand by getting followers to tag your brand, it needs to be explicitly stated in your guidelines.

Locate the Ideal Hashtag

A great hashtag is a foundation for any engaging Instagram contest. In the absence of this, there will be no connection between the generated content and the contest itself. What this implies is that hashtags can help in developing contest or brand recognition by acting as a tool for driving participation or sharing.

However, the problem is that it can be difficult to develop the appropriate hashtag. If you are going to include a timeframe for your contest, you need to develop a hashtag that you won't want to utilize recurrently. Also, many people create hashtags every day, and this might make it a tedious task to get an appealing and unique hashtag.

To aid you in creating the ideal fit for your contest hashtags, the following are a few guidelines to consider:

- Brief: Develop a hashtag that remains in the mind of followers. The easier it is to read and identify your hashtag, the more ideal it is for your contest.

- Significant: Ensure any hashtags you are creating relates to the product, services, or name of your brand. If you decide to go with something general, already with a lot of crowd, it may be challenging to determine the individuals taking part in your contest.

- Unforgettable: There is a huge possibility that users will come across adverts for your contest beforehand. What this implies is that your hashtag has to be easy and catchy enough for users to remember it later on. Put efforts into ensuring your hashtag is easy to write, not difficult to search and appealing enough. Stay away from difficult spellings and a strange choice of words.

- Global: Put your audience in mind. Do all of them use the same kind of words or speak one language? If your audience is global, ensure you exercise caution in using terms specific to a particular region which may confuse others from other areas.

- Uncommon: Investigate before picking a hashtag. Are a lot of individuals utilizing your selected hashtag for other uses? If this is the case, you may want to find something else.

Put a Theme in Place

Lots of contents on Instagram are based on UGC. For this reason, it is vital for you to choose a theme, so your audience understands the kind of videos and pictures they have to post.

Preferably, you will want to go with a theme that goes with your product, services, or market. However, you can leverage on seasons, holidays, and events that go with your brand or product.

Determine How You Will Select the Winners

A major aspect of a properly-structured contest is letting your participants know the way you will choose your winners. Many contests winners are chosen using one of the following ways: A jury or by votes: Let's check out how both choices work:

- **By Votes**: A great method of making your contest go vital is to get participants to contend for the most number of likes. If the incentive is great enough, individuals partaking in the contest will be keen on sharing their posts with their friends and loved ones across numerous channels so they can get the highest amount of likes. This approach aids in boosting your reach of audiences. However, this can also affect your contest negatively. This is because you may face the possibility of individuals using "Like bots" to get themselves fake likes. To ensure there are no issues here, you need to place specific guidelines that prevent participants from doing this.

- **Jury**: This method is a much better option than using votes. Using this method, you select a set of professionals to determine the winner as opposed to depending on a voting system. Regardless of the option, you decide to go with, ensure you explicitly state the method you plan to use so participants would know in advance. Lots of brands combine both options to decide the winner.

Pick the Right Reward

When you want to determine the reward for the contest, you need to reflect on your budget, target audience, and the kind of goals you have in place. Don't forget that by requesting your audience takes part in the contest, you are requesting they make a particular action. Similar to other efforts like this, the incentive they stand to gain has to be more than the energy and cost they need to partake in the contest. While not too many people may be awed by the chance to win a free pair of shoes, many of them would be eager to go out of their way for something like an exotic holiday.

The prize should correlate to the action for entry, but should also be in line with what your target interest is interested in. To determine this, ask yourself this question: What would my target audience be keen on having? You may come up with a huge list of responses to this if you don't consider the budget. Yes, many people will be eager for a free trip, but this should not be the focus. The objective is to determine a prize that is relevant and significant to your brand. Many brands take advantage of giveaways, free services, free products, among others. But, it does not hurt to be creative when making a choice.

Develop Terms and Conditions

Remember that when developing a competition with an incentive attached, you must go along with a few legal guidelines. The laws applicable to you may be dependent on your location or the individuals you give the chance to partake in your contest. This means you need to reach out to your legal practitioner for assistance in putting your terms and conditions in place. It is vital for you to create a terms and conditions page.

A few terms commonly added include:

- Rules guiding how to enter

- Rules guiding how a winner is selected

- Contact details and the name of the promoting brand

- Contest dates

- The rules guiding individuals that can partake in the contest

- The date the contest will end, and the winners would be announced

- The time frame for winners to give feedback and get their prizes

- Information about how the prizes will be sent to the winner or claimed

However, you need to go through the promotion guidelines put in place by Instagram to ensure you are in line with their rules.

Do Lots of Promotion

Now that everything is ready, you need to engage in serious promotion for your contest. So what are the ideal platforms to begin your promotion? The good news is that there are a lot of avenues to use. However, below are a few of them to pick ideas from:

- Your website: Write a blog post on your website, including the contest details, and use it as a point for redirecting users to the landing page of your contest.

- Social media platforms: There is no better place to promote events than social media. Take advantage of all your platforms to ensure your garner as many participants as you can to your contest on Instagram.

Chapter 12
How to Get the Help of Influencers on Instagram

Investing in digital ads can cost a lot of money. This is the reason why promoted posts and endorsements by influencers on Instagram has become more recognized. Besides, as stated by statistics, influencer marketing has one of the most ROIs in comparison to other online promotion techniques.

For this reason, if you want a fast method of getting your brand out there, you need to get the services of a micro influencer. But before we move any further, let's check out what influencer marketing is all about.

Influencer Marketing – What is it?

Influencer marketing is a technique for marketing that has to do with the partnership between brands and popular pages or personalities. Akin to ambassador programs and celebrity endorsements, Instagram marketing capitalizes on the loyal following and massive audience of an influencer. They are typically paid to make posts on Instagram. However, there are situations where the influencers will partner with brands, in return for a few of their products.

Well-established influencers can cost a lot and typically have a following which could get into millions. This may not be budget friendly for brands on Instagram that have just begun. In this case, the option is to go with a Micro-influencer, who does not have as many followers but gets high rates of engagements from their followers.

Why Instagram Influencers?

Marketing on Instagram is quite effective, and this is not shocking. Now, the traditional means of marketing has become quite invasive, while the new strategy of contacting customers via influencers has been verified to be more efficient. Influencers have a high amount of social power among their followers who see them as reliable and trustworthy.

In contrast to the conventional digital ads, which is a one-way form of advertising, promotions, and endorsements by influencers offer an open channel of communication with their followers. It is almost similar to word of mouth (WOM) marketing, which remains a very effective method of marketing today. Related to this, influencer marketing can get across to customers in a more welcoming and approachable manner.

How Does It Work?

Marketing on Instagram with the help of influencers is not as difficult as you may believe. It does not include any platform for campaign management; neither does it consist of any complex ad bidding or buying systems.

To start influencer marketing, all you have to do is:

- Locate an influencer who has followers that aligns with the target audience of your brand.

- Leave a message when you find the influencer of your choice

- Agree as regards payments or gift in kind as compensation for his/her endorsement of your product or brand.

When making a deal with your chosen influencer, ensure you have a time limit in place and utilize a distinct hashtag and code which the influencer will include in their post caption. It is an easy strategy to make sure that you can monitor the influencer marketing campaigns and determine how effective numerous influencers are. Now that you know how it works, how do you find the right influencer for your brand?

Finding the Best Influencers for Your Brand

To find the right influencer, the following are a few tips that can help:

Determine What You Require

Before you even contact any Instagram influencers, you need to have clear goals in place for what you want to achieve with your campaign.

Is your aim to:

- Promote a particular sales event or product?

- Do you want to grow your followers?

- Are you trying to generate brand awareness?

Providing answers to these questions is vital for putting a budget in place and directing your search for the ideal influencers. Note that if you choose to collaborate with a micro-influencer, you won't be privy to the same level of control a traditional ad campaign offers you. This means you will have to let the influencer develop content that aligns with their distinct style and viewers' preferences.

In the end, being keen to provide a bit of creative freedom will make it less difficult to locate influencers and develop a profitable campaign.

Now, with these in mind, you can now begin the search for your ideal influencer.

Search Using Hashtags

It is crucial to find an influencer who is relevant to the niche of your brand. Luckily, the search function Instagram offers makes this very easy to search for your ideal influencer. To get the best result, run your search using hashtags.

Use numerous hashtags that are related to the niche of your brand or organization to assemble a list of prospective influencers. When evaluating the results, pick images that you find appealing. Normally, Instagram shows posts that have the most engagement first, and this is a great way to locate high-quality influencers.

Check out every profile on your list to see how properly it aligns with the goals you have set in place for your brand. Take note of the rate of engagement, their frequency of posts, and if they usually post content that aligns with your niche.

Look for Bloggers

Bloggers can offer your brand a broad range of marketing opportunities. This is because well-established bloggers, in addition to making guest posts and running affiliate marketing, usually have a huge following. To find them, all you need to do is run a quick search on Google, specific to a particular industry to aid you in finding the best influencer for you.

As soon as you have located the best list of bloggers you can find, all you need to do is find their Instagram handles on their website or determine if they will make suitable micro influencers for you. If they do, then the next step will be to reach out.

116

Even if a specific blogger you would have loved to collaborate with does not have the following you are after on Instagram, it is never a waste to locate them. There is a huge possibility that if you make a connection with them, you can still use them to develop content and build trust in your audience.

Look for Those Who Are Open to Collaborations

Because a micro-influencer has a huge following, it does not mean he is available for collaborations or sponsorships. Luckily, lots of influencers offer vital signals in their profile to help you point out if you can collaborate with them.

Now, lots of micro-influencers will put up their contact details on their profile, to make it easier for prospective ad collaborators to reach them. Taking it a bit further by reading the signs will prevent you from wasting valuable time contacting those who don't want to collaborate.

Look in Your Followers

You may not know it, but your present followers on Instagram could be a very valuable resource for finding the right micro-influencer. This is the case so long as you are ready to put in the work and observe.

The people who follow your brand do so because they love what you do, and for this reason, you may not have to put in extra effort to persuade them that it is worth promoting your service or product. They like your brand already!

A lot of your followers will be keen on promoting your brand if you offer them a free sample product or other incentives. However, you need to do your screening the same way you would do normal influencers; **they should have** no less than 1,000 followers, posts that relate to your niche, and an interactive audience. If you know how to find the right influencers, but still have no idea of how to approach them the right way, you may never get any influencer to collaborate with you.

Approaching Instagram Influencers the Right Way

As we covered earlier, you need to investigate your chosen influencer before you collaborate with them. Taking it a little further, it is a great idea to follow them on Instagram and their other platforms. This will let you know the way they engage with their audience. If you are satisfied with what you see, the next thing is for you to directly engage them.

Your pitch and ideas for your campaign should be in place. Then you can contact them via their page on Instagram. Most times, you will find a link to a website where you can reach out to them. If this is not the case, lots of serious influencers place their contact info on their bio.

Running an Influencer Marketing Campaign

Now, Influencer marketing is now very recognized. Its popularity got so high that Instagram released a new feature known as Brand Partnerships, which caters to brands and influencers.

If you decide to or not to use this new feature, the impact on your campaign may not be so high. However, if you do use it, remember that there are a few partnership policies you need to go with. You can find them here. Ultimately, the vital thing is the technique you use in managing and approaching your strategies in Instagram influencer marketing. To aid you in starting, below are a few steps that you should follow:

Determine Your Audience

The very first thing to have in place even before contacting an Influencer is to have a detailed idea of your target audience. Ensure that the followers of your prospective Instagram influencer closely aligns with your audience.

Another way to do this is to split your audience into numerous groups. For instance, if your brand offers innumerable products to women you can search for influencers in precise niches in the lifestyle space of women like fashion, hair care, makeup, accessories, etc. All of the influencers can then assist in the promotion of various products offered by your brand.

When you categorize your audience, you can reach out to micro-influencers and possibly enhance your rate of engagement and ROI. Also, it will give you the chance to focus on a relevant audience centered around particular products.

Locate The Appropriate Influencer

To find your influencer, use the options we covered above. You can take it further by employing the services of tools like the Keyword tool. To use this, head to the PEOPLE function and input a topic or keyword pertaining to your brand. Then copy out the Instagram influencers from the result. As a recap, searching with hashtags, checking out blogs, and looking into your followers are also great ways to find influencers.

Next, go through each of them and choose only those that are relevant to your brand. If you find suitable choices, check out their pages to see if they suit your needs and make a choice. Picking those with a reasonable amount of following, with high rates of engagement and the same niche as you, will have a lot of impact on your campaign.

Reach Out to The Influencer

As we covered earlier, reach out to the influencer via his/her DM or contact information. They are also humans looking to make some money, so ensure you are polite and professional in your approach.

Measure Your Results

A great campaign for Influencer marketing is incomplete if you don't measure and track results. Regardless of the kind of influencer you decide to go with, or what your payment agreement with them is, you need to be aware of their performance.

By doing an analysis of their numbers like click-through and engagements, you will get a better understanding of which influencer provided better results for your campaign. With the information you get, you will be able to alter your campaign to make sure things go more seamlessly.

Below are a few tips for measuring and tracking your Influencer marketing campaigns on Instagram:

- Utilize a hashtag or unique code to keep track. The influencer includes this in his/her post caption.

- Use bit.ly to shorten links. This will give you the capacity to monitor click performance. This only works for arrangements that need the influencer to place your links in their bio.

- Make a spreadsheet for tracking. You can do this on Google Sheets or Excel. Then, you add various metrics like Clicks, Impression, Follower Count, and Engagement. With this document, you will have the capacity to monitor your campaign more comprehensively, particularly if you are working with lots of influencers.

Create a different landing page for your promotion on Instagram. After creating the page, install a Google Analytics tracking code. This can be a very effective option if you are running a special campaign.

Influencer marketing is something you can use on numerous social media platforms. You can use it to sell a product, promote a brand, or build your page on Instagram. It is certainly something you should take advantage of if you want your brand to grow higher than it is presently.

Chapter 13
How Does the Instagram Algorithm Work?

The algorithm is a deciding factor of who views your published content and who doesn't. This applies to both SEO and social media. However, these algorithms tend to change frequently, which makes a strategy that was effective before becoming obsolete. For this reason, you need to continuously advance as well.

When it comes to Instagram, especially, posting frequently using the appropriate hashtags won't imply that your content will get to the relevant audience. Rather, you will have to reflect on how to work around the algorithm to diversify your approach to marketing on Instagram. In essence, the value of the algorithm is something you can't underrate, which is what makes it something vital to consider. In this chapter, you will learn the way the Instagram algorithm works and how you can work around it to achieve the best results. Now that you understand what the algorithm is, how exactly does the Instagram algorithm function?

How Does the Instagram Algorithm Function?

The new Instagram algorithm determines the arrangement of the posts that will be viewed by users when they scroll through their feed. Using certain signals, it gives priority to posts, pushing those that are relevant to the top and offering them a high level of visibility, while the less relevant content is moved to the lower end of the user's feed.

Instagram published some information in June 2018, showing a few elements that the algorithm capitalizes on when ranking the content on the feed of users. Although it is vital to understand that the recent algorithm could be altered later in the future, there are still some major factors used to rank a post which you need to consider in your Instagram strategy. They include:

- Connection with the user: If a specific user has engaged with a host of your previous content, they have a higher probability of seeing your recent content. This allows for repeat and continuous engagement on your content, which is vital for the development of loyal followers.

- Level of interest shown by the user: This signal is dependent on if the user engages with other accounts and posts similar to yours when they go through Instagram. In essence, any user who shows interest in content related to yours, has a higher tendency to see posts you make.

- How recent the post was: Previously, Instagram utilized a sequential feed. However, this is no longer the case, but that does not mean the timing is not a factor to date. Posts which were recently uploaded will be pushed above the feed, while less recent posts will come up further below.

Instagram also shared some additional considerations which are vital; they include:

- If users follow numerous accounts, your struggle to get to the top of their feed will be more

- If you are not on the top of the feeds of users who don't stay so long on Instagram or check out the application, the chances of your content been seen are lower.

- In comparison to Instagram business accounts, personal accounts are not instantly at a disadvantage when it has to do with organic reach.

Now that you understand how the Instagram algorithm works, you need to learn how you can alter your strategy to get to more of your clients. To do this, the steps below may be of help:

Don't Focus On Reach Alone, Relationships Matter Too

Loyalty from your audience alongside continuous interaction from those who follow you, now has a higher level of importance, since it will be able to provide you with a spot at the top of their feeds.

There are ways to establish these relationships using your content, some of which include:

- Reminders that urge users to share their opinions and things they feel and offer you a chance to begin a discussion with them.

- Uploading posts that help build engagement, like Instagram contests or tag-a-friend post that urge users to leave comments.

- User-generated content concerning your brands that have been posted by your followers. In addition to aspiring more UGC, users might tag you in the posts they make and further develop your Instagram presence.

However, if you want to make headway on Instagram, you need to think beyond your posts.

Leave Comments On Posts from Brands and Users Relevant to You

You can also interact with the people on their posts to develop relationships beyond your posts, by making relevant and engaging comments on content from influencers pertinent to you, prospective clients, and related organizations.

Also, leaving posts on more established accounts that have a huge following can provide more visibility to your profile and comment as well. Take a look at accounts that the audience you are targeting has a probability to follow, follow these accounts, and become a part of the conversation. If you decide to go through this route, be authentic, and ensure you make relevant comments. Don't just leave non-specific responses or sales pitches. Show the personality of your brand and engage in a relevant manner.

You can take it a step further by turning on post notifications for certain accounts. This will ensure you can leave comments promptly, enhancing the possibility that it will get visibility, thanks to the focus of Instagram feeds on recent posts. To achieve this, it is essential that you are a follower of the account. Tap the three dots at the right-hand angle of the application and hit "Turn on post notifications" to begin getting push notifications the instant they upload a new post.

Upload Posts During Peak Periods

Since the recency of posts is still a major consideration for where your posts will be placed in the feeds of your followers, you need to exploit it. It, not a bad idea to get a huge level of engagement when your post first goes live, and it will inform Instagram that this a post that would love to be seen by a higher number of your followers.

To enhance the possibility of each post you make, make efforts to upload content when your followers are most active. Refer to the steps in Chapter 6 to find the right posting time for you.

Leave Responses to Comments When They Are New

When you leave responses to as many comments as you can, you will enhance your number of comments while boosting further replies. Additionally, it increases your probabilities of getting more engagement while the potential reach of your post is at its highest.

When you respond to comments, it can lead to additional comments from the main poster. Even something as simple as a thank-you can go a long way. However, in some circumstances, you can begin conversations which give you substantial engagement that will aid in increasing the reach of your posts and other posts in the future.

Use Community Hashtags to Get to Users Who Are Active

Instagram hashtags can aid in increasing your reach by ensuring you come up in significant searches. However, if you want this approach to be efficient, you have to pick hashtags that your audience uses in searching for content as well as other users.

Community hashtags, in particular, are quite active. Although they may not have as many posts as the other well-known hashtags, they are already being shared and explored by numerous groups on Instagram who are in search of ways to create connections with others that have an interest in that movement, topic or community.

From here, you will obtain views that can provide you with clicks via your engagement, profile, and prospective followers. Although these relevant hashtags will differ according to industry, it is easy to find them because they define your perfect customer and are constantly filled with new posts related to your niche.

Repost Already Existing Content to Add a New Feel

If you have issues generating adequate content on Instagram to get more pull in terms of traffic, or you want to ensure that particular content gets seen by as many users as possible, a great way to go is to repurpose previous content, especially as your follower base increases.

This will push you leading content to the top feed once more. In addition, those who missed it when you initially posted it will get to enjoy it this time. Although many brands just delete an old post and post it how they previously shared it, repurposing content works differently.

If you have no idea of how to properly repurpose content, the methods below can help:

- Include a caption different from the one you used previously

- Make a video of the past post images

- Integrate new designs into the picture. You can easily do this if you edit the image of the previous post using the various filters available to you on Instagram.

- Use popular hashtags to share your existing content once more like #throwbacktfriday

It can save you a lot of time if you repurpose content. However, you should not rely on it. Remember to diversify, and go through your feed to get rid of duplicate content. Users will still have the capacity to check your previous posts, and you want to make sure they don't come across the same image numerous times.

Utilize Stories to Gain Attention

A lot of marketers focus on Instagram stories because the algorithm they use is not the same as the ones used in the posts on your feed. It is also an amazing method of interacting with your followers and enhancing loyalty. This leads to an increase in engagement on your stagnant posts, which in turn leads to additional reach.

The following are ways to do this:

- Incorporate hashtag stickers to your branded hashtag

- Encourage engagement using interactive stickers

- Share Stories uploaded by other users

- Urge you, users, to put on post notifications

When you do this in the right manner, like subtly sending a reminder to users, it can prove to the algorithm how significant your brand is to your community. Those who turn their notifications on, in addition to seeing more of your content, will have more likelihood of engaging with your posts.

Make Sure Your Posts Are Amazing

Instagram has made it known numerous times that producing amazing content is the only method of increasing the feed ranking of your content. However, Instagram's major appeal has always been the unstated rule that you need high-quality pictures.

So if you want better engagement, this might mean you need to take a different approach. You can get the services of an experienced photographer and find out what you can learn. You can also download new tools that can increase your knowledge of editing photos.

Remember to Develop Relationships

If you want the best Instagram has to offer, you need to do more than regularly post content. Rather, it is vital that you also pay attention to developing a relationship while keeping communication with users on your pot and beyond them.

Social media algorithms tend to change. However, if you take the innovative and change with them, you will learn that there are numerous methods of getting the audience you desire.

Chapter 14
Tracking your ad success on Instagram

After you have set up your ad campaign and published it, you can relax and hold on for the outcome of your ad. However, it does not stop there. To ensure your Instagram ad is a success, you have to monitor and measure the results and determine if it is a success. Ensuring your ads remain a success after you have put them up, is also as vital as publishing them in the first instance.

In this chapter, you will learn how you can do this using the Facebook Ads manager and some of the most important metrics you need to track.

Instagram Ads Reporting – How to Get Started

Shopify states that posts on Instagram have a 1.08% rate of conversion, which in comparison to other social media platforms like Pinterest with (0.54%), and Twitter with (0.77%), is on the extremely high side ("Instagram Ads Reporting and Optimization – Guide to 10x Results", 2017).

If you are a marketer or a brand trying to break into Instagram, this is certainly great news for you. However, you need to learn how to view the precise ad results of your campaigns on Instagram. The least difficult means of accessing your Instagram ad reports is to sign in the Facebook Ads Manager. Here, all of your campaigns currently running and those that have been completed in the reporting page will be visible.

Remember that you require an Instagram business account to view comprehensive campaign reports. When you navigate to the reports page on the Facebook ad manager, you will be able to categorize your ads by objectives, dates, and so on. You can also zoom in to a particular campaign to measure how all the ads you put up are performing.

To choose a campaign, you need to click on the checkbox which you can find before the campaign's name. Next, you can head to the Ads tab and Ads set to view how every unit is performing in a specific campaign. If you want to see more metrics, find your way to the Columns page, and choose another report setup.

Campaign Breakdown

Coupled with the campaign metrics that will be displayed in your Ads Manager reports, you can further elaborate on your Instagram ad results with the help of the Breakdown menu.

With the breakdown function, you will be able to screen campaigns using:

- Time: days, weeks, or months

- Delivery: Gender, device location, time, age, browsing platform

- Action: video sound, destination, conversion device, video view type, and so on.

You can choose one criterion from all sections — for instance, one from delivery, and another from time, and so on.

With the report breakdown by placement, you can compare the placement of your Instagram ads against other ad placements, which are currently active. In addition, it offers you answers to lots of other vital questions like:

- What target countries perform the best?

- Which regions come with the most Instagram ads cost?

- What device users have the highest rate of conversions?

- What time of the weekend or days offer the highest conversions at the least cost?

To further split your campaigns using various criteria, you need to select one Facebook Campaign or more. Then, pick a criterion from the breakdown menu. If you are going through the Facebook Ads reports for the first time, it can seem very confusing, because there are lots of data you probably don't know how to summarize. The tips we covered above can make it less difficult, but with experience, it gets much easier.

Vital Metrics You Need to Track

To further ensure you are successful, below are some essential metrics you need to keep track of, so you can see how well your ads are performing.

Relevance Score of Instagram Ads

A relevance score is a number between 1-10 which aids you in understanding the reaction some specific ads is getting from your audience. This metric is calculated by Facebook for each of your ads, using the three core factors below:

- Is your ad performing properly? Are you getting the conversions you optimized for?

- Negative feedback from those who come across your ad. For instance, when a person hits, "I don't want to see this," the instant your ad comes up.

- Positive feedback from those who come across your ad. For instance, clicks, views, app installs, and so on.

You can view the relevance score of your Instagram ads in the Facebook Ads Manager reports. All you have to do is pick "Performance and Clicks."

When you have a relevance score between 1-3, it implies that the Instagram ads are not really relevant to the audience you are targeting. But a score of 6 and above can drastically reduce your cost of advertising. This is because Facebook will give them priority over other ads in competition with yours, and would deliver your ads to a much broader audience. To enhance your relevance score, you can update your Instagram copywriting or ad design. Better still, you could employ another form of Instagram ad targeting.

Number of Conversions

The number of ad conversions and impressions is also another important metrics you need to look into. If you notice any ad that seems to be doing very well in regard to the rate of conversion and cost per click, but only delivered a few conversions, then it is not an ad which is doing well. To view the number of Instagram ad conversions, clicks, and impressions, as before you need to pick the "Performance and Clicks" section from the menu.

Conversion Rate

Your conversion rate is another important campaign metric you want to monitor in your Instagram reports. Conversion rate shows how large a fraction of the users who check out the ad and convert on your bargain. You define the conversion in the setup phase of the campaign. This could include signups, link clicks, purchases among a host of others.

To see the average rate of conversion of your ad, you will have to do some simple calculation. Divide the number of conversions by that of ad impressions, then multiply the sum by 100.

(CPC) Cost Per Conversion

Similar to your conversion rates, if your ads are having a great click-through-rate, but don't convert, then you won't attain any new clients. This is why the CPC is your most vital campaign metric. It lets you learn the amount a conversion actually costs you.

To see the CPC metric, you have to define the conversion for your ad campaign during the process of setup.

Instagram Ad Frequency

This displays the amount of time an average user in your audience has viewed your ad. If the frequency of your ad gets beyond 4 points, it implies that members of your audience have viewed your ad numerous times and have probably gotten tired of it.

To find out your ad frequency, navigate to the Facebook Ads Manager, select a campaign, and pick the Delivery view in the reporting page.

From here, you can view a campaign's ad frequency, and set your chosen ad level in the column for reporting.

How Does the Data in Your Instagram Reports Help You?

The ability to get information concerning how your ads are performing at a comprehensive level is of huge benefit. You can utilize your reports in optimizing your ads in numerous ways, which include:

- The kinds of ads that have the best or worst performance

- The period of the day, your audience is at its peak, or when your level of engagement is higher, to enable you to take advantage of the dayparting options Instagram provides.

- The ad creative that has the best or worst performance

- The demographic areas with the best or worst performance

- The countries with the best or worst performance

In essence, every option you are provided with when setting up your ad is something you can experiment with. You are also privy to a look at the metrics that have the best and worst performance. With this information, you can prevent a campaign from falling apart by getting rid of the ad or device with the worst performance, or any measurement your report proves is setting your campaign up to fail.

Chapter 15
Growth Strategies for Brands on Instagram

Now, Instagram is one of the top recognized social channels on the net. As we have mentioned earlier, it is a good place for individuals to share, create, and connect with their friends and the brands they love. It is known that 80% of Instagram users follow a business on the platform.

Similar to other social channels, a brand with the goal of getting the best Instagram has to offer, requires a decent amount of following. An increase in the number of followers means enhanced credibility, more engagement, and a better presence online.

However, the issue is that growth on Instagram goes beyond a game of numbers. Organizations are leveraging on the $6.48 billion value of profit churned out from Instagram each year by creating genuine connections with individuals who pay a visit to their pages ("US AD Spending", 2019). However, if a brand is aiming to grow, it is vital for the growth to be organic. Let's learn why below.

Why Must the Growths of Brands On Instagram Be Organic?

Many people have tried purchasing brands at some point in time. These include celebrities, influencers, and even politicians.

As a newcomer on Instagram, convincing your customers that you are valuable to them when you have only a few followers can be very difficult. But, if you have a huge amount of followers, your credibility seems to spike. However, going with the crowd and doing what others are doing won't get you anywhere. When you pay for followers, it means numbers are the only thing that will be added to your account. In essence, the individuals you are posting content for, won't take any practical action on your page. They won't share your content, like your pictures, or purchase your product. Also, buying followers breaches the guidelines of the IG community, which implies that your account could be at risk of a purge.

So, if purchasing followers is out of the question, how do you make yourself unique from the other active organizations on Instagram? The solution to this is quite straightforward; you need to learn to increase your number of followers organically. Below, we shall be covering some strategies that can help you grow on Instagram organically.

Growth Strategies for Brands on Instagram

As a brand on Instagram, there are lots of growth strategies you can implement to increase your follower count. Some of these include:

Make Quality Posts Frequently

Instagram, as we covered earlier, had the most levels of interaction in comparison to other social media platforms. Your followers are available to create connections with you. However, you have to provide something for them to engage with first.

Users are always in search of timeliness and stability from the businesses and brands they follow. Additionally, the Instagram algorithm puts your presence on Instagram into consideration when trying to determine where to place you on the Explore Page. But, when you begin to plan a consistent schedule for posting, you have to attain the right timing as we have covered earlier. It won't be of any benefit for your followers consisting of professionals if you make posts during the day when they would be at work.

It will be essential for you to do your research into information like the habits of your audience to ensure your schedule is ideal for you. Also, to recap, if you don't have time to manage your growth on Instagram consistently while running your business, you can take advantage of some of the tools for scheduling we listed earlier. When you prepare posts before-hand, it makes sure you have a continuous influx of content available, even when you are occupied with other activities.

Offer Your Audience What They Desire

Similar to other authentic strategies for getting organic growth, getting organic growth on Instagram requires amazing content. In the end, if your aim is for people to follow, like, and interact with your page, then you will have to upload content that they find appealing.

So, what methods can you use in determining what your followers anticipate from you? Below are a few ways to do so:

- Observe competitors that have target audiences similar to yours: determine the type of content brands in niches similar to you are posting and point out everything that amasses a high level of engagement. For example, do brands in your niche get better outcomes when they make video posts instead of typical images?

- Monitor the trends: monitor the profiles of influencers and customers in the space as you to determine the trends they have been following or hashtags they are utilizing. Doing this will provide you with an understanding that brings the most engagement among your followers.

- Track your performance with the help of a tool: there are a host of tools like Sprout Social, which you can use to follow keywords that are bringing you the highest amount of traffic and engagement among your followers. This way, you will learn why your posts with the top performance are working and implement the results in your other posts.

If you are having issues picking the appropriate content to get organic growth on Instagram, a great way is to find out from your followers the form of contents they would want to see. You can use the poll feature offered by Instagram to get feedback and ideas from your present customers.

Try Out Various Forms of Media

Do not forget that Instagram goes beyond images alone. Although the images you post each day can help you build your reputation and personality on the platform, you can shake things up a little by checking out other options as well.

For instance, more than 60% of the ad impressions gotten on Instagram are from videos (Vrountas, 2018). Trying story ads increases click-through rate, marketing recall, and buying intent simultaneously. As video content keeps on ruling on Instagram, it can be a great choice to make your feed diversified. Also, with the advent of IGTV, there are more avenues for exploiting videos. To do this, try out the following:

- Behind the scene footage which introduces your team members and develops organic relationships

- Question and Answer sessions with influencers to enhance how credible your brand is

140

- How-to content that showcases your product's or service's distinct appeal

Interact with your followers

Similar to all other social media platforms, Instagram has to do with engagement. A lot of brands in the search for Instagram growth, make the mistake of ignoring the social aspect of marketing on social media.

When you post the appropriate content, at the right moment in a consistent manner, it will draw in increased attention from your audience. However, it is the way you communicate with the people in your audience that will transform a typical visitor into loyal fans of your brand.

When you respond to a question, comment, or reply to a DM, they will all aid you in the development of more meaningful relationships with the people you follow. It is not essential that you reply to every mention or message; all you need to do is be as active as you can. Your followers recognize that you have a business to run; however, all conversations you have with them will be appreciated.

Enhance Your Hashtag Tactic

Hashtags are not to be undermined when it comes to attaining organic growth on Instagram. They can effectively induce engagements on your post. Also, users can follow IG hashtags, which makes it less difficult to broaden your reach using the appropriate tags.

However, the guidelines for using hashtags have changed, as now, IG places more emphasis on tags that are relevant and provide your followers with distinct value. Now, it is not possible to expect results if you post the same ten tags on each of your photos. Rather, you have to locate the appropriate blend of tags for every post that can enhance your image.

To get the best outcomes, experiment with:

- Branded Hashtags: Utilize the name of your organization or a distinct tag to build your brand's engagement. More than 60% of the hashtags on Instagram are branded (West, 2019).

- Current tags: Take a look at the tags that are coming up on the explore page of Instagram. Do any of them apply to your content or brand? Consider including them to your posts to make your reach broader.

- Location tags: Posts incorporated with geotags get more engagement than others. This is as high as 79 percent. To find geotag, check out the top left part of your post (West, 2019).

- Recognized hashtags: Although #TBT and #Love, are well-known hashtags and may be difficult to get good rankings with, they can still fit in some forms of content. Try including a few well-known tags to your stories and images.

Boost more User-Generated Content (UGC)

If you are having issues attaining measurable growth on Instagram, you can look into your present followers for help. Customers have a higher likelihood of purchasing from a brand their peers suggest to them. Also, tags and mentions from your client can aid you in reaching a new audience that you typically won't have found yourself.

There are numerous methods of developing UGC. An easy option is to begin a competition using a branded hashtag. Offer your clients the opportunity to win a special price if they upload and share a picture of themselves using your product, tag people they know in the comments, or follow your profiles.

The instant you pick a victor for your contest, you can gain access to a higher number of user-generated content by requesting that your customers showcase their prize or post a review on their profile. Do not forget that giveaways require:

- An appealing reward

- A way of keeping track of entries

- Promotional tags and branded hashtags

Grow Some Influence

It can be difficult to learn how to organically boost your followers on Instagram. It takes a lot of time to get genuine progress because you have to get the respect of a customer and show how credible you are in a competitive marketplace. A great method of instantly pushing your efforts ahead is to take advantage of the influence someone in the same niche as you already possesses.

Using Influencer Marketing is a seamless method of amplifying the voice of your brand on Instagram. With the appropriate influencer, you capitalize on the trust already in existence between an Instagram user and his/her followers, to broaden the reach of your brand. Locate influencers in your niche by looking for hashtags in your industry, and start to develop a relationship with them fast.

Do not forget that there is a proper way to reach out to influencers. Don't just go in and request for a shout-out immediately. Rather, leave comments on their contents, mention them on posts you make and send them free samples of your products. Ultimately, you and the influencer should come to an agreement.

Get Attention Beyond Instagram

Lastly, don't forget to push traffic back to your profile on Instagram from other online locations. Don't conclude that the individuals who follow you on Twitter and Facebook are also aware that you have an active Instagram account. Leave links redirecting users back to your posts on Twitter and Facebook, place your branded hashtag in emails and take a screenshot of images on your Instagram profile to be included in your blog posts.

The higher the level of attention you draw back to your Instagram page from other avenues on the web, the more the reach of your brand. Also, when you develop your presence on other platforms, you may enhance your trustworthiness enough to get an opportunity to be verified on Instagram.

A few methods of promoting your IG channel on other platforms include:

- Being a guest writer on blogs significant to your audience

- Including details of your Instagram profile in your email campaigns

- Turning in press releases alongside links to your account on Instagram

- Mention your posting links and hashtags on other platforms of social media.

It is not easy to determine how to build your followers organically. But it does not mean it can't be done. The top accounts on Instagram invest a huge amount of effort and time in creating it. This is the reason many brands choose to take the easy way out, one of which is to purchase followers.

Don't fall into temptation. Remember that even though this may initially feel like a great idea, it would have no positive effect on your business. Rather, ensure you pay attention to careful content development, organic growth, and continuous measurement.

Chapter 16
Spying On Your Competitors Ethically

Competition is vital in every area of life, and Instagram is not exempted. Even if you believe you have no competition, the truth is that some other individual out there is offering the same service as you. So never underestimate the requirements of individuals as they are the same in all aspects of the globe.

So if you are the only one providing a service in a specific region, remember to look for likely competitors around you or in other countries aside from yours. But how can you determine what your competition is doing on social media, specifically Instagram? How do you learn about their behaviors or strategies? Are these answers even essential to you?

Put simply; the answer is yes. You should have an interest in all of these details and understand each of them so you can use the results you attain to build your page on Instagram. In this chapter, you will be learning how to spy on your competition regardless of where they are situated. But first. Let us look into why you need to spy on your competitors ethically.

Why Do You Need to Spy?

Simply put, you have to learn about your opponent if you want to do better than them. It is also a means of getting inspiration and ideas for how you can promote your brand and grow it. Below are a few ways ethically spying on your competitors can assist you:

- Learn where they excel and where they don't: By spying on your Instagram competitors, you will be able to learn the areas they are excelling in and how you can do better from them. Also, by learning the areas they have no success, you will be able to pick lessons from their errors and ensure you don't do the same things.

- Find out the kind of content they are sharing: By spying, you will learn if your competition has better content than you, or if they are getting more engagement on Instagram than you do. Then, you can learn about the kind of content to provide and which to stay away from for the best engagement. This way, you eradicate the need for wasting time alongside trial and errors when you want to engage with your audience since you have an insight into what works and what does not.

- What method of promotion do they use for their brands? Spying on your competition can show you the marketing strategies they currently employ. You will also learn if it is providing them the results they desire. Since they are in the same niche as you, and you both are after the same target audience, whatever works for them would most likely work for you. Better still, you can improve their strategy and be better than they are.

- Learn what their activity on social media is like: What is their level of engagement? When you spy on your competition, you can learn the amount of engagement and if it is more than yours. Also, you will learn if their number of followers is increasing at a faster rate than yours and the reason behind this. With the results, you can learn what you are doing wrong and step ahead of the competition.

Now that we have covered these, below are a few ways to spy on your Instagram competitors.

148

Take Advantage of Unique Tools That Monitor Your Competition on Instagram

There are numerous methods of spying on your competition, but you can take advantage of tools to help you with it. Using a tool like Brand24 can help you take the work off your hands while you channel your energy to other areas.

Develop a profile and begin to create a project for your brand. In addition to this, create one for your competitors. It is not difficult to utilize and is an easy and amazing method to spy on their activities, their mentions, and the effect they have on their network. Brand24 lets you pick the profiles you want to follow for your competition and your brand. For instance, utilize Instagram as the network of your choice, and you will be able to view all of the mentions the users convey all through social media that have to do with your competitors and your business.

Take advantage of tools to take the work off your hands so you can pay attention to your technique, so you can ensure it is more enhanced than that of your competitors. Some other examples of some of these tools include:

- Sprout Social

- Phlanx

- Social Blade etc.

Follow Your Competition On Instagram

When you follow your competition on Instagram, you will be able to monitor how they communicate with their audience. Also, you can benefit from the tricks and tips they don't directly offer. However, remember to use another profile to follow them, because they will know you are spying on them if you use your brand profile.

By following your competitors on Instagram, you see what they share and like. You also see how they respond to contents. Even if the competition is in another county, the idea still stays the same, and you can easily tap from them.

It is vital to observe the way your competitors behave naturally with followers they know or don't know. The idea is to see the value they offer their audience.

When you follow your competition on Instagram, you learn the following:

- The kind of posts they employ to reach their clients and audience on Instagram. Various organizations employ a host of descriptions and slogans in their posts. But when looking into your competitors, it is vital for you to learn the keywords they integrate into their posts. Aside from keywords, you can check out the terms and wordings of their posts and how long their captions are. Ideally, for the best engagement, captions should consist of 138-150 characters.

- Frequency of posts and best posting time. Understanding the frequency of posting by your competitors is vital. By following them secretly, you can learn their posting times and see the level of engagements they are getting.

The outcome of your investigation will help you learn when to post your content. You will also find out the kinds of filters they are using and get inspiration to create something better on your page.

Follow their Instagram Stories Using a Fake Account

As we covered above, you want to be subtle about it when following your completion on Instagram. They may know who runs the business profile, so it's best to use a random account and follow their Instagram Stories and posts. This is more essential when it comes to Instagram stories since they will be able to tell who checked out their stories.

However, remember that any form of content, regardless of if it is a story, photo, or video is tailored to a precise audience. This means you can easily adjust it to fit your audience as well. But, you need to remember not to copy and repost it directly. Instead, get inspiration from it. Check out the kind of audience they have, what they engage with, and who they follow; then you develop a similar content for Instagram.

Run a Search for Their Branded Hashtags on IG

In addition to following their accounts, you have to do some investigation of your own. Follow posts made by your competition and take note of the precise set of hashtags they utilize. Look through Instagram for the hashtags to learn who else is utilizing it and create connections with them.

To succeed when marketing on social media, having a branded should go a long way. If you know this, your competitors will certainly know this too and would have branded hashtags. To make your task easier, you need to learn the hashtag they capitalize on the most. When you do, run a search for it on Instagram, learn how they interact with those who follow them, and how the audience responds. You can observe your competitors to learn the appropriate hashtags you can integrate into your content, so it gets to a broader market.

It is also vital to find out the active users or influencers who upload posts on Instagram with the hashtag of your competitors. This will keep you informed on the hashtags to employ on your posts. If you utilize the right mix of hashtags in your posts, you can make it easy to discover your brand, which in turn enhances your engagement on Instagram.

Websta and Pixlee are great tools that can help you with it. Also, you can use the search explorer on Instagram. This is a very seamless way of learning how your competition acts on Instagram and how they are viewed by their audience.

Takeaway

Competition is not a bad thing. It makes you want to get better than you are. If you were the only one providing a service without any competition, you won't strive to become better and will continue to repeat the same thing over and over until your audience gets tired or bored.

However, with the presence of competition, you become aware of how you can better serve your audience. You also get the desire to understand what their wishes are and how you can make it happen.

If you understand how to deal with competition, and use it for your benefit, it will be more of a positive thing for your brand instead of negative. Spy on your competition ethically, observe how they act, respond and communicate with their audience, adapt and do better than they are doing, and with time, you will grow to lengths you never imagined possible.

Conclusion

Instagram has proven to us how valuable visuals can be. It has provided numerous amounts of brands and individuals an amazing platform to market themselves and their brands.

It is only essential that you exploit what Instagram offers you and you are bound to get to where you desire. If you are just signing-up on Instagram for the first time, the truth is, you will have to channel a huge amount of effort to make yourself unique.

In this book, I have covered a lot of information that you can take in and implement to make your Instagram journey an easy one, even if you are a newcomer to the platform. All that is left is for you to remain creative and come up with unique strategies to pull loyal fans and followers.

So why wait? Take the step today.

Bibliographies

22+ Instagram Statistics That Matter to Marketers in 2019. (2019). Retrieved from https://blog.hootsuite.com/instagram-statistics/

33 Mind-Boggling Instagram Stats & Facts for 2018. (2019). Retrieved from https://www.wordstream.com/blog/ws/2017/04/20/instagram-statistics

Balakrishnan, A., & Boorstin, J. (2017). Instagram says it now has 800 million users, up 100 million since April. Retrieved from https://www.cnbc.com/2017/09/25/how-many-users-does-instagram-have-now-800-million.html

Chi, C. (2019). When Is the Best Time to Post on Instagram in 2019? [Cheat Sheet]. Retrieved from https://blog.hubspot.com/marketing/instagram-best-time-post

Clarke, T. (2019). 22+ Instagram Statistics That Matter to Marketers in 2019. Retrieved from https://blog.hootsuite.com/instagram-statistics/

Dunn, B. (2019). Retargeting - How One Campaign Generated Me 16,900% ROI. Retrieved from https://ppcmode.com/traffic/retargeting

Enterprise, F. (2019). Social Media Case Studies & Client Stories | Sprout Social. Retrieved from https://simplymeasured.com/blog/adidas-wins-with-instagram-how-the-brand-doubled-followers-in-under-3-months/#sm.000o9am0pymue7t10aq2nohh77wzk

Friedman, M. (2015). Which Photo Filters Get the Most "Likes" on Social Media?. Retrieved from https://www.harpersbazaar.com/culture/news/a10979/yahoo-georgia-tech-flickr-photo-filters/

Global Instagram user age & gender distribution 2019 | Statistic. (2019). Retrieved from https://www.statista.com/statistics/248769/age-distribution-of-worldwide-instagram-users/

Global Cosmetic Products Market Will Reach USD 863 Billion by 2024: Zion Market Research. (2019). Retrieved from https://globenewswire.com/news-release/2018/06/22/1528369/0/en/Global-Cosmetic-Products-Market-Will-Reach-USD-863-Billion-by-2024-Zion-Market-Research.html

How much is the travel industry worth? Try US$5.29 trillion - Travelweek. (2019). Retrieved from http://www.travelweek.ca/news/how-much-is-the-travel-industry-worth-try-us5-29-trillion/

Instagram Ad Costs: The Complete Updated Resource for 2018. (2018). Retrieved from https://adespresso.com/blog/instagram-ads-cost/

Instagram Ads Reporting and Optimization – Guide to 10x Results. (2017). Retrieved from https://karolakarlson.com/instagram-ads-reporting/

Johnson, T. (2019). The Ultimate Guide To Amazon Baby Products. Retrieved from https://www.cpcstrategy.com/blog/2019/05/amazon-baby-products/

Price, E. (2012). Facebook Buys Instagram for $1 Billion. Retrieved from https://mashable.com/2012/04/09/facebook-instagram-buy/

Pet Care Market Size Worth $202.6 Billion By 2025 | CAGR: 4.9%. (2018). Retrieved from https://www.grandviewresearch.com/press-release/global-pet-care-market

Social Media Case Studies & Client Stories | Sprout Social. (2019).
156

Retrieved from https://simplymeasured.com/blog/adidas-wins-with-instagram-how-the-brand-doubled-followers-in-under-3-months/#sm.000o9am0pymue7t10aq2nohh77wzk

Schmidt, S. (2018). 4 Pet Industry Trends to Watch in 2018 and Beyond. Retrieved from https://blog.marketresearch.com/4-pet-industry-trends-to-watch-in-2018-and-beyond

Smith, C. (2019). 250 Amazing Instagram Statistics. Retrieved from https://expandedramblings.com/index.php/important-instagram-stats/

Study: The most popular Instagram filters from around the world. (n.d.). Retrieved from https://www.canva.com/learn/popular-instagram-filters/

Taylor, C. (2012). Instagram Passes 50 Million Users, Adds 5 Million a Week. Retrieved from https://mashable.com/2012/04/30/instagram-50-million-users/

Top 10 Successful Hashtag Campaigns That Created an Impact. (2019). Retrieved from https://medium.com/@unboxsocial/top-10-successful-hashtag-campaigns-that-created-an-impact-3605f4d6e5fc

The Best Time to Post on Instagram By Day, Niche & More. (2019). Retrieved from https://www.sharethis.com/best-practices/2018/03/best-time-to-post-on-instagram/

US AD Spending. (2019). Retrieved from http://bluemoondigital.co/wp-content/uploads/2016/12/eMarketer_US_Ad_Spending-eMarketers_Updated_Estimates_and_Forecast_for_2015%E2%80%93 2020.pdf

Vrountas, T. (2018). Why Instagram Video Ads May Be a Good Fit for Your Brand. Retrieved from https://instapage.com/blog/instagram-video-ads

West, C. (2019). 17 Instagram stats marketers need to know for 2019. Retrieved from https://sproutsocial.com/insights/instagram-stats/

Book 2: Facebook Marketing

The Handy Guide

Introduction

I want to thank you for choosing this book, Facebook Marketing Step by Step: The Handy Guide.

Facebook marketing is a brilliant way not just to start but to also grow your business with limited risk or investment. However, this is possible only when you are aware of what needs to be done to effectively market on Facebook. Do you want to learn about Facebook advertising and marketing strategies? Do you want to learn how to start creating, running, and analyzing ad campaigns? Do you want to leverage Facebook's resources to develop your online brand? Well, if yes, then this is the perfect book for you.

With the help of this guide, you will be armed with all the essential knowledge you need to succeed in the world of Facebook marketing. You will learn about the fundamentals of Facebook marketing, how to use Facebook Ads Manager, the steps involved in Facebook advertising, the different analytical tools available to measure your progress, how to use Facebook Pixel, the best metrics to track, and a variety of different tips to create high-quality content.

Even if you don't have any prior knowledge or experience in online or social media marketing, you don't have to worry. This book will act as your guide and will help you achieve your social media marketing goals and learn how to advertise your products on Facebook to maximize your returns successfully.

So, if you are eager to learn more about marketing and advertising on Facebook, then let us get started without further ado.

Chapter One
Introduction to Facebook

Facebook is the largest social network in the world with over 1 billion active users. Apart from this, content on Facebook also attracts over 1 billion likes per day, along with millions of comments on various posts. It is easy to see why Facebook can help businesses grow and why it would benefit you to start using it for your own business.

Facebook is very user-friendly, and while it is used by many people for entertainment purposes, it is also used by many businesses to promote their brands. One of the great things about Facebook is how easy it is for you to connect to your target group via Facebook. You can group your target audience and send them group messages. You can share content with them to promote your business and ongoing sales or promotions.

But just because you can effortlessly reach an audience doesn't mean marketing on Facebook is as simple as posting a picture. There is an art to Facebook marketing which must be mastered. Before mastering it, however, it is important to understand what can be gained by marketing on Facebook.

About Facebook Marketing

When Facebook was originally founded, its goal was to cater to college students primarily. However, the use of Facebook is no longer limited to college goers, and it has certainly come a long way. Everyone seems to use Facebook now, regardless of age, gender, or location. It reaches a truly global audience and, with its extensive user network, builds connections that otherwise would have been nonexistent. The size of its platform has revolutionized the way businesses and brands of all sizes can interact with customers.

The marketing revolution started by Facebook was unprecedented, particularly because Facebook was not the first social media site to take over the internet. During the initial stages of the social networking revolution, Myspace was quite a big name in the field. Between 2003 and 2006, the site had around 100 million users, and by June 2006, it had more visitors than Google.

Then Facebook was created, and everything changed. By 2008, Facebook had become more popular and had more users than Myspace. The increase in Facebook's popularity meant a decrease in the number of users of other social networking platforms, so companies considered investing in marketing on Facebook.

But that decision came with some uncertainty. Marketers were worried that Facebook would lose its steam like other social networking sites. However, Facebook has proven to be much stronger than past social media sites, and even after over a decade, it is still considered to be among the most popular and frequently accessed social networking platforms. The kind of access Facebook provides businesses with is quite unheard of. You can reach a global audience without having to worry about any geographic barriers or differences in time zones. The conventional methods of marketing like advertising by using billboards certainly don't offer the reach like Facebook does.

Facebook marketing is a simple concept. It's the creation and active use of Facebook as a communication and contact channel to attract potential customers. To facilitate this process, the platform offers numerous features that are available to the average user. Facebook users have the tools to create custom profiles or even business pages for companies, organizations, or groups that want to promote a product, service, or brand. The tools allow for a much larger marketing campaign that other options such as billboards or email blasts.

Facebook offers an ever-increasing audience, as well. Right now, there are approximately one billion active users who represent approximately one billion potential customers. That's an audience that even a large multinational company would have struggled to reach in the pre-Facebook days.

The platform ensures that you can quickly reach this target audience without having to worry about any geographical restrictions, and the large number of Facebook users basically guarantees that you will be able to find others interested in what you have to offer. While the number of people interested in your business may be small at first, if you start posting high-quality content that is engaging and interesting, then you will soon see that the number of people following your page will increase. People want to interact with an active and engaging page, so maintaining a lively page will only serve to benefit you.

In the past, marketers stressed the importance of maintaining an active website, and while that still applies today, it is important to realize that your Facebook page is as important to the business as a website. Regardless of whether you represent a small business or promote your brand, it is safe to say that part of your customer base is active on Facebook.

Facebook marketing is unique in that it is a type of marketing that can be used by anyone who has access to the internet. It is not restricted to a certain field or niche. Brands that sell various types of food, electronics, household items, restaurants, and any other type of product can be advertised on the platform. It is also not restricted to only companies or brands that generate high profits. Even small companies that may not generate much profit are able to use the platform.

With its interactive platform, Facebook helps turn passive users into active customers who can interact with you in ways that previously would have been impossible. Access to Facebook is open to everyone, and the intimate relationship it can build between customer and business is truly unlike any other.

Using Facebook

The first step to mastering Facebook marketing is simple: Create a Facebook profile. It only takes a few minutes to register to create your Facebook profile. Once you register, you will be redirected to your homepage. There you can customize your profile and make it as attractive as possible.

After setting up a Facebook profile, you need to move on to the next step, which is to create a dedicated Facebook page to promote your business or brand online.

Facebook allows you to create a separate page for your business. This means that you can create a page and send links to all your target audience to motivate them to subscribe to your page. This is quite different from a regular profile you create because you cannot "friend" anyone here. People merely need to follow your page.

The goal of a Facebook page for your business is to give you a place where you can provide your customers with information about your products, product descriptions, and any other promotional activities. It will also allow you to interact with customers and consumers and to actively engage your audience in your business.

Creating a page for your business is easy, but there are several steps to follow:

Step one: The very first step of the process is to visit facebook.com/pages/create. Once you click on the link, you will be directed to a page where you can start creating a Facebook page.

Step two: It is important that you carefully fill out all the fields displayed on the screen. Try not to leave too much information blank. You will need to select the type of business, add a profile picture, write a short description of the business, create a username, and fill in the details in the "About" section.

Filling out the details carefully while creating your Facebook page can make all the difference between a good and a mediocre page. It is important to take your time when creating the page to ensure that the information you publish is accurate. Including the correct details, such as address and phone number, will make it easier for potential clients to find your page.

Step three: Choose the right category for your business so people can easily find it. You must consider all the different business options offered. These can range from a local business, artist, band or celebrity, brand or product, company or organization/institution, entertainment, or any other cause or community. Go through these options and carefully select one that suits your needs. By doing this, you can ensure that other users can find your page easily.

Step four: The next step is to create a URL, which is the identifying web address for your page. It is a good idea to include your business name in the URL you create so that the users immediately know where they are being directed when they see the link. You need to make finding your page as easy possible if you want to make the most of marketing on Facebook. The simple way to do this is by selecting the right URL and adding the appropriate information.

Step five: Now that you have created your page, it is time to start actively using it. Take some time to publish posts or pictures relevant to your business. For example, if you are a restaurateur, you can upload the menu to the page, post pictures of the food items, inform the users about all the different dishes you serve at the restaurant, and tell them about your special menu. Making this information easily accessible to your followers will encourage them to continue following the page, and it may even prompt them to take advantage of what you're offering.

Step six: After following the above steps, your Facebook page will be ready to share with a wider audience. Before inviting others to like and follow the page, be sure to check your information to make sure everything is correct. Make any needed changes to make sure your page is as professional as possible. You should also ask a few friends and family members to look at the page and suggest any changes you may need to make. Once everything is done, and you make the necessary changes, you can send invitations to other users. This is as simple as clicking on the "Community" tab and selecting the option to invite your friends to like your page. You can enter a person's name and then select the "Invite" option. An invitation will be sent to them.

Step seven: If you have a website for your business, the next step is to add a "Like Us on Facebook" icon to your site. This is important because you need to tell your target audience that you exist on Facebook. You will also need to copy your URL and paste it on all of the other social networking sites that you use for your page. This may include Instagram, Twitter, or LinkedIn. You should also place the link as your email signature so the users know your business is active on Facebook.

Step eight: There is no point in creating a Facebook page if you don't use it. Now is the time to become active and start interacting with your audience. Posting interesting content will ensure your audience is engaged and interested in your page. Be sure to vary your content. For example, if you started with pictures, you should start to add some videos. These videos may include demonstration videos or other topics that you think your audience will enjoy. Remember to cater your content to the people who matter most: your followers.

Step nine: Some brands and businesses tend to hire dedicated teams for

168

managing their Facebook accounts and pages. However, this is optional because you can run your page yourself. Hiring help will only increase the costs involved, and you will have to set aside time to find an ideal social media team. That's why many people prefer to manage their own pages.

If you want to make the most of Facebook marketing, then you must concentrate on the content you are posting. Make sure you are using only high-quality images or videos and are using appealing descriptions for the content you are uploading. Don't just keep uploading pictures and text; instead, try to mix it up a little. Start posting videos, gifs, and stories. You can even take advantage of the ability to go live with Facebook Live. There are several helpful features that Facebook provides, but you must use them correctly in order to fully reap the benefits. This will help you ensure your target audience is interested in the content you are posting.

Step ten: Establish a posting schedule and stick with it. Even if you are not interested in publishing posts daily, you still need to post consistently. You can choose to publish on different days, but be sure to select posting times based on when most of your audience is using Facebook. When you do this, it increases the chances of your posts appearing on the newsfeed of your target audience. Remember to check the posts even after you have posted them. Interact with your audience and answer any questions they may ask. The point is to be interactive and tell them what they do not know about your business and products.

Step eleven: Use your Facebook page to try to increase the traffic to your website. You can easily do this by posting the kind of content you know your target audience will like and appreciate. You can also link certain posts to your website, which will encourage people to visit the site. Try to stop thinking from the perspective of a marketer and instead think like your potential audience.

Step twelve: Take advantage of different Facebook groups to promote your page. Groups differ from Facebook pages because they allow group moderators to restrict who can and cannot join the group. Groups also allow you to send messages to just the people who are members of the group. If you join another group, you can inform them about your page, and you can easily direct traffic to your page. While it may seem effective to join as many groups as possible, it's best to stick to pages that are relevant to your niche to ensure you are reaching people who will be interested in what you have to offer. For example, if your Facebook page is related to fashion, then it doesn't make much sense to join a group about finance because members will most likely not be interested in what you are selling.

Step thirteen: Place paid advertisements on your Facebook page to attract visitors. This step is optional, but it will increase traffic on your Facebook page. Simply put, paid Facebook ads are ads that you create through Facebook and then place strategically in an effort to positively impact your business. This may mean increasing downloads of a certain app or promoting an ongoing deal. The idea of making your own ads may be intimidating, but you will learn more about how to master ads later in this book.

Those are the primary steps to follow when creating your Facebook page. Keep in mind that your work doesn't end there; it's really just starting after you create your Facebook page. You must keep updating it regularly and consistently interacting with your audience to encourage them to keep supporting your business. It is also important to understand the following components of a Facebook page and the available tools.

Account name and bio

If you want to create a Facebook page, you must first choose a name that is recognizable and short. You can use the brand name and include the region you wish to target if you have one. For a profile picture, it's best to use some type of graphic de   sign or a recognizable character, such as a logo.

For instance, the Facebook page for McDonald's can be easily recognized by users because of the name used and the logo. The Facebook page name is McDonald's, with special pages created for different regions. The profile picture is the classic McDonald's icon, the double golden arches.

Like McDonald's, you must opt for a name and profile picture which will help your target audience recognize your brand.

The bio on your page is a short description of what your business or brand is about and the purpose you serve. Placing the link to your business website in the bio is the simplest way to redirect the traffic to your website. Therefore, it is important that the hyperlink included in the biography redirects users to the right landing page. Before publishing your page, make sure the hyperlink works properly.

Create awareness

Creating awareness of your brand is essential, and this is done through effective marketing. You don't have to go into this blind, however, and you can use other brands' successful marketing campaigns to help you understand how to be successful. One way to do this is to figure out your niche, or target, audience.

Once you find the niche audience you are targeting, check for a similar page or people who are influencing that niche. A simple search on Facebook will help you identify the influencers in the niche. For instance, if you are in the restaurant business, try searching for "restaurants" on Facebook. The results will show you a list of the top trending posts, tags, accounts, and places related to the search. Model your marketing approach after the most successful ones in your niche.

It's important that you analyze the composition and style of the photos and videos taken by such influencers in your niche to get an idea of the kind of content you must post. The awareness about your business on Facebook will increase when you create content that leaves a good impression on the users.

It is important to create a strong foundation based on innovative and engaging content. This contributes to the success of your brand on not just Facebook but any other social networking sites you use. Keep in mind that people use Facebook to access original and engaging content that adds some value to their lives. Users don't access Facebook to see ad campaigns. So, if you want to market on Facebook, you need to tread the fine line between being a good marketer and maintaining a social profile. You will learn more about this in the subsequent chapters.

Promotions

Running contests and promotions is a great way to engage your customers. If you're running contests or campaigns, it's best to use Facebook to reach a wider audience. When distributing prizes, it's better to scale the prize based on the engagement shown by the users. If a lot of effort is required, it is better to distribute prizes that will increase the rate of participation and the interest of participants. For instance, Eggo, a frozen waffle company, hosted a two-part contest on Facebook. It was essentially a recipe contest where the entrants had to submit their best recipe for making waffles. The second part of the contest was that the followers of the Eggo page had to vote for the recipe they liked the best and the winner was awarded $5000.

One of the simplest and most basic contests is the Like and Comment contest. Users can like and comment on photos or videos posted on your brand page, and they enter a contest that is valid for a short period. You can use Facebook Insights to track entries and contact the winners. You can change this contest by asking users to take a picture or use a specific phrase. For instance, you can host a contest where the participants need to post a picture using a specific phrase or hashtag you created. You will learn more about Facebook Insights in the coming chapters.

When a contest ends, you can publish the winning posts while announcing the winners. When you declare winners and give them a prize which can be something as simple as a shout out, it will encourage other users to participate in any future contents you host.

When you start attracting the audience and engaging with them by responding to their comments or acknowledging them for liking your content, you are essentially working on developing a good relationship between your brand and the other users or your target audience. Using original content is the best way to increase your reach. If you are using any user-generated content, then please ensure that you seek the permission of the creator before using such content to avoid any legal issues.

Community management

If you are active in a Facebook group, you can increase your brand awareness. You will get to know about the brand's community better when you follow those who are the spokespersons, influencers, partners, and advocates of the brand. However, if you track and respond to comments, you can extend the ongoing conversation. It is always good to reward your followers for being loyal to your brand. Giving them simple benefits such as discounts, promotional codes, gifts, and product samples will make an indelible impression.

Facebook analysis

If you want to measure the effectiveness of the content you post, you need to examine two metrics: reach and engagement. It is important to keep track of other data too, but these are the key performance indicators that help assess brand performance on Instagram.

Reach: This is the total number of people who have seen all the content you have placed on your brand page. The most popular content on Facebook will easily show up when you search for a topic or keyword associated with such content. By installing certain benchmarks for the kind of content you want to post, you can improve the content you publish and easily increase the number of subscribers. These benchmarks will help you create content that appeals to the audience of your brand. If your profile has hundreds of views, you can get more people to follow your brand, increasing your reach.

Engagement: On Facebook, engagement is measured by the number of likes and comments on a post. You can track different types of data, such as filters and their performance, content, and style of the content that has attracted the most attention, to increase your engagement.

You will learn more about analyzing and tracking the important metrics on Facebook in the coming chapters.

Facebook Apps

Facebook is also available on mobile devices. The user interface is extremely simple and easy to use and will help you navigate through the different aspects of a typical page. Most users check their newsfeed to update themselves about all the posts posted by those they follow.

Facebook also has various applications that can be useful for anyone running a social media business portfolio. These applications were made for the sole reason of helping businesses have a good social media presence.

Facebook Groups is one such application. You can create a Facebook group for your product, business, or just your staff. The main purpose of this application is to manage groups easily. A Facebook group helps communicate with all those who are integral to your business or will help you in some way. You can review all the posts and deal with the members; you don't have to open your Facebook app every time for this.

The second app is called Facebook Page Manager; it's a must for anyone trying to increase the reach of their page. Managing a page is not simple, and it requires a lot of work. It can be hard to deal with page-related tasks on the regular app. Page Manager has a brilliant and easy to use interface that is perfect for anyone managing a page from their phone. It allows you to customize your page, deal with the settings, and fix any other issues just from your phone. The app really lets you work on the go because you can manage the pages on your mobile phone, use Page Insights present in the app to check how your page is doing, and make any necessary changes. For instance, the app shows information like the content with the highest engagement rate, and you can use this information to create content which will appeal to your target audience.

How Facebook Helps Businesses

Facebook as a whole is a great way to grow a business, but it also offers smaller features that further allow you to improve your marketing techniques.

Quickly reach the target audience

With Facebook, you can reach many people in no time. It's not just about sharing information about your product with all those people; it's about reaching your target audience as quickly as possible. Facebook helps you to reach your target group in the shortest possible time, and it also allows you to customize your audience.

Ease

With Facebook, people can easily find your company, your brand, or the products and services you offer. It seems almost everyone has a Facebook account, regardless of their age, and many of those people spend a lot of time browsing the various product pages on the site. Having a Facebook page makes it easier for your audience to find you. This is easier than trying to find the address of your corporate website on the internet.

Chat rooms

Facebook offers the opportunity to communicate with your potential customers and existing customers on your Facebook corporate page. Any complaints and problems can be rectified immediately. This helps to maintain clarity in business practice, build trust, and build customer loyalty.

Low cost

You can share real-time information about your products and services without worrying about the costs involved. Free advertising is the best form of advertising.

Viral advertising

Those who like your Facebook page can easily share your page and even post about their experiences on their Facebook accounts. If you can influence other users about your Facebook page, brand, business, or activities, then they can, in turn, influence their followers about the same. This tends to have a cascading effect when it comes to online marketing, and it will help increase the traffic to your pages. This is what viral marketing is all about, and Facebook will help you achieve this goal.

Target customers

You have the opportunity to focus on those people who are interested in what you are offering. Because these people willingly become part of your Facebook page, you can offer them special notifications about future offers, promotions, etc. before other customers hear about them. For example, an invitation to a launch event may be sent to hundreds of people. However, granting a special discount to all previously registered individuals will certainly attract more people.

The fact that there are more than a billion active users does not mean that everyone likes your page. It makes no sense to target every user on Facebook. Instead, it is sensible to target the audience who will be interested in your brand or business, and Facebook helps. Once you understand this, it's not that difficult to create a marketing strategy.

You can easily get likes and focus your ads to target such users by posting quality content. If you have a local business, you need to position your ads to reach potential customers who live within 10 to 15 miles. Advertising may be a little expensive, but the likelihood of reaching your potential customers is higher. Placing advertising on TV or even in a local newspaper is not only expensive, but you also may never know if it has reached your target audience or not. With Facebook ads, you can know whether or not you've targeted your ad correctly.

Social proof

Social proof is a psychological occurrence where people tend to copy or imitate the actions of others in order to portray the appropriate behavior according to a situation. One example of this would be using products endorsed by celebrities.

Social proof is very important to any business because it can persuade customers to buy a product simply because other people are using it. People can also be persuaded to like, comment, or share one of your posts because others have done the same. The number of likes, shares, and comments you receive helps increase your online presence. It also may give you the confidence you need to work on a wider range of products or services. All these likes and promotions can also help you determine if the public approves of what you are doing.

Understand customer behavior

Understanding customer behavior means you understand what things attract the attention of the audience and which ones make them take action. This will help the company to develop a marketing and advertising strategy that takes into account the needs and sympathies of its customers. You can use Google Analytics to understand customer behavior.

Understand data

Facebook helps track a lot of data related to your business efforts on the platform. By analyzing this data, you can easily determine whether your marketing and advertising efforts are paying off or not. This is very useful when it comes to making decisions because it ensures that all the decisions you make will pay off. The data are designed to help companies get a detailed analysis of how their site is accessed. Data can change the marketing strategy of any business significantly, and you will learn more about this in the coming sections.

Gather new customers

If you want to secure a long-term and sustainable business, then you need people to do more than just like your company's Facebook page. What will you do if your Facebook page fails and customers are unable to interact with you on it? You should be able to connect with your customers in ways that go beyond Facebook. Smart companies collect potential customers by capturing email addresses so they can communicate with their customers outside of Facebook.

All of this usually happens through competitions, giveaways, and newsletters. However, you must be careful about how you use all of this information. For example, you should not spam your fans or customers by sending them multiple emails a day. Email them once or twice a week, and make sure the promotional content you provide resonates with your target audience and the people receiving the emails.

Reduce your marketing costs

You do not have to spend anything to open your own Facebook page for your brand or business. If you like, you can hire a graphic designer to design your profile and cover, but this is not necessary. You can take a picture of your business, and it will be fine. Until you start paying for advertising to get likes on your page, you do not have to spend anything to customize your page.

Compared to regular advertising, advertising on Facebook is quite cheap, and it helps you to reach a wider audience. The number of people participating on your page also increases the visibility of your page. This will help you to attract more attention without doing a large amount of work. Targeting your ads to people who are interested in your product can help reduce your costs.

Use Facebook Insights

There are some people who are really good at analyzing data, and then there are some people who tend to struggle. A nice perk with Facebook is that you don't have to worry about number crunching for analyzing data because Facebook Insights will do this for you. It simplifies the entire data process. The information provided is not only easy to understand, but it also provides what is truly useful for business owners.

Insights provides information about the number of likes a page has received, how much coverage posts and pages have received, a summary of page activity, and more. You also have the capability to check how a particular post works, the overall demographics of your followers, and other important metrics. The results of the Insights analysis are easy to analyze, and you do not have to understand any technical issues. When you compare this to traditional advertising techniques, you will realize that Facebook Insights makes advertising quite simple. All of this data will be useful as you develop your marketing and advertising strategies since you can create better ads to will target your ideal audience.

Sets brand loyalty

In addition to building a customer base and selling products, you can increase brand loyalty with your Facebook page.

What exactly does brand loyalty mean? As you continue to provide valuable and engaging content, your followers remain loyal and ignore your mistakes.

Nowadays, people often turn to social networks for searching for brands or businesses to start buying from. If your subscribers find that your brand or business is sufficiently active and responsive on the Internet, they're more likely to engage with you than they would be with a company without a Facebook presence or a poorly managed site. In this age of technology, the Internet has become an important part of our lives. Social networks are an effective substitute for real-time conversations. People usually turn to social networks to exchange opinions about different things. If your brand is represented on social networks, your chances of winning new customers and retaining existing ones are higher.

Increases your web traffic

An intelligent Facebook site owner uses the Facebook page to direct traffic to the website. If you want to be a good marketer, you need to do more than just get viewers on your Facebook page. You need to publish links along with messages to encourage traffic on your site. A good content strategy should include publishing links to your website. You can post information about the content associated with your website twice a day and combine it with a few other carefree posts to attract an audience. If you have the right placement strategy when posting content on Facebook, you can increase your web traffic.

SEO advertising

SEO stands for search engine optimization, and it is vital to growing your online presence. Simply put, it helps increase the quality as well as the quantity of website traffic by increasing the visibility of the website or the webpage to the users of a specific search engine.

SEO and its relationship with Facebook are a topic that is often discussed. Some people believe that the information you provide in the About section of a company page can be searched for on Google, but that belief hasn't been confirmed or disproved. If you're doing a simple Google search for your business page, your Facebook business page will be one of the first results you see if you have a Facebook page. In marketing, it helps if more people can find you easily. Everything is good for your business, and a Facebook page will help to improve your visibility on the Internet.

Mobile access

Most Facebook users access this social platform through their mobile devices, including smartphones and tablets. The nice thing about the Facebook page is that Facebook will do all the hard work for you. This means that your Facebook page will automatically be optimized for viewing on the desktop or a mobile device, depending on which device the user is accessing. The exception is a tab that displays custom applications on your corporate page that appear when you access Facebook through your desktop, but not on mobile devices (unless you provide mobile-friendly links). So, by optimizing the Facebook page to be displayed on a mobile phone, you make the page more user-friendly. When users view their Facebook corporate page on their mobile device, they need to be able to easily find opening hours, address, ratings, phone numbers, and reviews, if any. You need to make sure your page contains useful information.

Competition

Facebook has a new feature that lets you keep an eye on the competition in the marketplace. This does not mean that you can view their offers or see their sales or results from different ads. However, this is a great way to see how your competitors and others in your niche are growing on this social platform. Going through the kind of content your competitors are using will help make it easier for you to understand whether the audience is responding to such content or not. If you see a strategy that works, then you can implement it too.

You have the option to customize your channel. You can add a list of your competitors and track their results. Facebook also provides you

182

with a list of similar business deals near you that you can activate by clicking the "View Page" option. You can choose five or more pages according to your wishes. If you look at the pages in this release, you'll see if there's any activity or user interaction on the page. In that case, you can check what they are doing. This will help you develop new ideas that can work for you as well.

Facebook for Business

Facebook offers numerous resources for business, but here are some of the most useful.

Facebook for business

The first resource you need is Facebook for business. If this is your first attempt to use Facebook to promote your business, be sure to check out the Facebook for the Business page first. On this page, you'll find useful information on how to increase sales, increase brand awareness, and search for the latest updates and tools available on Facebook.

Advertiser support

Facebook is an amazing platform for reaching your target audience through targeted advertising campaigns. To find out where to start, visit the advertiser support page on Facebook. Any questions you have about advertising on Facebook will be answered on this page.

Training for advertisers

You will need to visit the Facebook Advertiser Training page to learn more about how Facebook can help your business succeed. Here you will find all the information on Facebook pages, Facebook advertising, best practices, and much more. There are about 34 e-learning modules on the Facebook Blueprint page that allow you to gain hands-on experience and practical experience on best practices and resources on Facebook. All you need to access this page is a Facebook account. You can even find specific online courses created specifically for your business that are available free of cost.

Video tutorials

To learn more about how to create brilliant videos for your Facebook profile or page and to understand how the videos work. you need to visit the video lessons Facebook page. This page contains various success stories and tutorials that will inspire you.

Creative tools and tips

Facebook is very popular with marketers and users but not a lot of people know how to optimally use this platform. This is especially true with ads. Many people understand that ads must be creative and attractive in order to engage an audience, but they don't realize that creating such ads is possible through Facebook. Many people have a limited budget, so they assume that Facebook ads are out of reach. But that's not true.

Facebook has created the Facebook Creative Shop. This is your one-stop-shop for all Facebook-developed tools that can improve the quality of your ads and reach a wider audience on a budget. The Facebook team is constantly working with the company to develop various tools, processes, and creative ideas to help it grow.

Guide for Advertisers

If you want to get expert tips on creating brilliant ads on Facebook, visit the Facebook Guide for Advertisers page. On this page, you will find all the information you need to develop effective and efficient ads on Facebook. Some of the topics covered here are ways to help you get more conversions or how to improve the visibility of your ads.

Advertising on Facebook differs based on your audience and your goals. By going through the different free courses available on the Facebook Business page along with all the different suggestions given in this book, you can start creating well-optimized Facebook ads.

Advertising policy

It is important that you are familiar with the guidelines for Facebook advertising. Before your ad shows up and you can connect to your audience, the ad you develop or your ad campaign needs to be in sync with Facebook's advertising policies. All necessary information is available when viewing ads on Facebook.

On the Advertising Policies page, you'll find a list of reasons why your ad can be disapproved and a list of all prohibited content. For instance, Facebook prohibits any ads related to gambling, the lottery, alcohol, and cigarettes, as well as ads featuring any drugs, weapons, arms and explosives, violent content, malware or spyware equipment, unsafe diet supplements, "adult" content, and counterfeit documents. Only if the ad complies with all these rules will you be able to start an advertising campaign.

Help Center

If you have questions about using Facebook for your business, you can find the answers to these questions in the Help Center. Here you can get useful information on topics like password management and problem reporting. If you have specific questions, you can post them on the help page, and the Facebook Help Team and other Facebook users will answer your questions. You can also read questions from other Facebook users. If you have any suggestions or feedback that you would like to share with the team on Facebook, you can post it on the Help Page.

Chapter Two
Fundamentals of Facebook Marketing

There are three main aspects of Facebook that you'll learn about in this section: target audience, engagement, and conversion.

Create a Target Audience

The importance of creating a target audience cannot be overstated. It is essential if you want to successfully market your product or business on Facebook. To do this, you need to understand how to best create that audience.

Set a routine

You need to make sure that the routine for publishing the content you select is appealing to your audience. Do you know your target group? If you do not know this, here are some questions that will help you understand your target audience.

How old is your ideal customer base?

Are you targeting a specific gender?

Where does your audience mostly live?

What type of content does most of your audience usually value?

What are the usual questions your audience tends to ask?

Use this knowledge to help you cater your content and posting schedule to what most of your audience prefers. You must determine a specific schedule for posting your content. If you have a structure, you can ensure that the content reaches the audience. Your goal is not only to attract your current users but also to encourage them to spread information about your business.

Search

Graph Search is a great tool to help you explore your brand's audience. If you do not have a well-established audience, you need to learn more about the users who visit sites that are related to the products or services you offer. The first thing you need to do is select two Facebook pages that are either your competitors or are similar to yours. Then you have to look for sites that appeal to their fans. For example, search for "pages that people like who like Nike and Reebok." The search results for this listing will help you analyze the content your audience is interested in.

Targeted ads on Facebook

All the information you gathered in the previous step must now be put to use. Whenever you decide to advertise on Facebook, you must ensure that your ads are well targeted. Therefore, make sure that they appear only on the pages of all the people who correspond to your ideal target audience. If you don't do this and you try to target all the users on Facebook, you will merely be increasing your marketing costs without much yield.

Premium content

You have to create content that is not only valuable but is also something that appeals to your target audience. You cannot expect to attract an audience unless you offer them something attractive. One way to do this is to offer them free premium content to stay true to your brand. For instance, if you have a Facebook business page for your restaurant, then the kind of content you offer must be related to your business or niche. If you start posting about politics on a page which was meant for promoting your restaurant, you will be turning your audience away.

Hashtags

The use of hashtags on Facebook has become very popular recently. Hashtags are phrases or words that are used to mark something as being related to a certain topic. They are preceded by a # sign, such as #advertising.

Hashtags are a great way to reach a wider audience. You can search for hashtags that currently are trending in your niche and use them to increase your reach. Use hashtags that are appropriate for the content you offer. Whenever a Facebook user searches for a hashtag, all pages associated with that particular hashtag are displayed in the search results. For instance, you can use a hashtag like #freshandyummyfood for promoting your restaurant business. So, whenever a user searches for this hashtag, your Facebook business page will pop up. This is a simple and effective way to improve visibility on the Internet.

Network

If you have not been online yet, you need to get started right away. You need to be able to look beyond Facebook if you want to promote your business and create a large audience. Collaborate with bloggers and influential people on other social networking sites to send links to your Facebook page. The simplest way to network is by using Facebook to message them or by contacting them on any other social media platform they are active on.

Engagement

Engagement refers to any interactions your target audience have with your business or brand on Facebook. It can be in the form of likes or comments on posts, by sharing posts or even by messaging on Facebook. The key to understanding engagement is realizing that once you have created an audience, your work doesn't stop there; it is just beginning. You must maintain your current audience while working to increase your audience. You'll need to learn how to increase Facebook's activity.

In this section, you'll learn about a few simple things you can do to increase your interest in Facebook.

Your personality

Social media is all about social. Nobody wants to interact with a media bot. Instead, you need to prove the identity of your company or brand in your Facebook posts. You need to make your business sociable for your audience because only then will they want to engage with it. The best way to go about doing this is by promptly responding to any comments or likes you receive on posts, by acknowledging your followers, or any other type of engagement along those lines.

Ask questions

If you want people to connect to your posts, the easiest way is to ask questions. You can ask your fans and subscribers specific questions and wait for their answers. You can ask them questions about everything, but make sure the questions you ask are not too technical. The idea is to make your followers talk. For instance, on your restaurant's business

192

page, you can post the picture of your idea of comfort food and ask the followers to comment with their favorite comfort foods. It is all about starting a conversation.

Images

A picture is worth a thousand words, and this is true on Facebook. You can send a meaningful message across by using multiple stories because images tend to look more attractive compared to the text. It will benefit you to take some photos to promote your business or brand and then post them on Facebook. It will also help your followers understand what your business is about. You can also start using Facebook Stories where you can post videos or pictures. Posting pictures related to your business, employees, and customers. Use more visual media instead of solely depending on textual posts.

Sneak peek

The amazing thing about using Facebook as a marketing tool is that you can promote your business without looking for too much advertising. You can post snapshots of employees, customers, your daily operations, behind-the-scenes work, or even information about an upcoming event. In a way, these pictures give your company a human feel, and that's what people want.

Specific content

You should pay attention to the type of content your audience responds to. If they don't seem interested in a specific topic, don't post it.

You also need to focus on posting content that will maximize the number of likes, shares, and comments. To ensure people comment, like, and share, you must once again focus on creating content which appeals to your audience. The more likes, shares, and comments you receive in your posts, the wider your potential audience.

Fan content

The easiest way to build relationships on social networks is by sharing other people's content. If you've ever come across useful content, even if it comes from other companies, do not hesitate to share it. Share the news with your subscribers. Everyone appreciates good and useful content, but do not prioritize posting any content over posting quality content.

Simple posts

Sometimes a simple text status can have a huge impact. You do not always have to share tons of information or long messages. A simple post does its job. No matter what you decide, have fun and don't always try to make the content about your business or brand. If you want your subscriber base to grow, you need to make the page interesting. If all you post is promotional material and ads, your audience will quickly lose interest and you will start losing followers.

Conversion

One of the most important indicators a social marketer can track on Facebook is the conversion rate. A conversion occurs when a person interacts with an ad you post and then performs an action beneficial to your business. It can also be viewed as the point where the user decides to switch from a normal browser to a customer. This can apply to an online purchase or even a call to your business. And the potential for a high number of conversions is vast considering that Facebook boasts over 650 million visitors per day.

For most marketers, the conversion is a top priority. A good conversion rate is an indicator of success. Remember, though, that the conversion is not always associated with purchases and actions of the driver. The goal of the campaign may be to increase the subscription to the weekly newsletter or to encourage customers to add more products to their wish list.

Luckily for businesses, Facebook is one of the best conversion platforms. In this section, you'll learn how to increase conversion and further benefit your business or brand.

Define a conversion event

Before you think about conversions, you must first decide what action people should take after viewing the ad. The different types of conversions that Facebook supports include viewing content, adding products to their wish list, starting the order, and purchasing. You can even create your conversion events if you have a specific goal. You cannot expect an ad to reach all your conversion goals, so you will have to create different ads to achieve different goals.

Do not forget the goal

There is a direct connection between the ad and the landing page, or the page or the website the link in the ad redirects the users to. The ad is only as good as the landing page. When you choose a location to convert, you need to make sure everything is ready and the ad delivers as promised.

There are a number of things you should consider when preparing your landing page. You must implement pixels (a code from Facebook that allows you to track conversion data) if you want to track an event. After you've determined the landing page, you'll need to add the Facebook Pixel code to track the event.

There must also be continuity between the ad and the landing page. For example, if an ad is for shoes and a landing page redirects a customer to a page about apparel, then the ad doesn't serve its purpose.

Today, many people do online shopping on their smartphones, so it makes sense to send traffic to your application. Therefore, you must optimize the application to increase the conversion rate.

Visuals

You must use attractive visual effects to attract your potential customers. The user's first impression of your company or brand is the design that they see, so you can think of the visual the users see as being similar to the way you would greet someone by shaking their hand when you first meet.

There are a few things you should consider when designing visual elements for advertising. You need to make sure that you do not clutter the images along with the text. A good idea is to save text on pictures. When you fill an ad with images and text, it looks chaotic, and there is a chance a potential customer will scroll through the ad.

Visual elements should also have a high resolution because all low-resolution visual elements give a bad image of your brand. Moving pictures are better than static pictures, so try using a GIF, or moving image, whenever possible.

Short and sweet

If the ad contains too much content, the conversion rate is very low, so you have to make a short and simple copy. Try to use personal pronouns (like us or we) to establish a relationship between the audience and the business. Avoid jargon and keep it short. A short text looks attractive, and too much text can be quite overwhelming.

Call to action

Conversion is the motivation to act. Therefore, you must insert a call to action in the ad. You can use active verbs such as start, search, explore, or even detect to increase your conversion rate. If you'd like to increase the number of purchases or subscriptions, you can use expressions like "buy now" or "register now."

Target group

When creating an ad, you must select a group you want to target. If you select this, Facebook will help you find more users with similar interests. This will allow you to further expand your audience and reach more people. The bigger your audience, the higher your conversion rate.

Optimize for conversions

By now, you have learned different strategies for optimizing or increasing your conversions. However, another option is to enable the "Conversion" checkbox on Facebook. Go to the "Budget and Schedule" form → "Delivery Optimization" section → and tick "Conversions." You will learn more about the optimization of Facebook ads in the coming chapters.

Format of display

You have to select a specific advertising format on Facebook according to the goals of your advertising campaign. Some formats can serve a particular advertising campaign better than other options. For example, Adidas used videos with the Facebook Collection feature to demonstrate the various Z.N.E Road Trip Hoodie features and reduce the overall cost of conversion.

There are some things to keep in mind when choosing an ad format. You can use carousel or group displays if you want to present some products or different functions. Ads with Facebook offers are a good idea if you want to publish special offers or discounts as an incentive to buy. If you want to use stunning visual effects and impressions that look good in full-screen mode, choose Facebook Canvas. There are numerous types of ads which we will discuss in upcoming chapters.

Facebook Marketing Tools

From the perspective branding, Facebook is different from other platforms in the history of marketing. It has more than 1.6 billion active users, offers international reach, free page creation, and is an excellent platform for advertising, regardless of your budget. Facebook can now run third-party advertising, which further increases the likelihood of success in this network. On Facebook, you can do everything from ads to promotions. Facebook marketing becomes easy if you understand the basics. There are many opportunities for marketers and advertisers.

Although marketing on Facebook is relatively easy, it isn't without its challenges. Many people lack enough knowledge to successfully use the platform. Facebook is pretty easy to use, and you certainly do not have to be a tech guru to understand this platform. Facebook simplifies the process by providing creation and management tools, but not many are aware of their existence.

Manually creating advertisements can be frustrating and inconvenient. Even if you have a really good idea, developing a separate ad on this platform is very time-consuming. This is a pretty big investment, especially for small businesses.

Another major obstacle that most newcomers to the Facebook marketing world face is that they depend on superficial numbers, such as the total number of likes or views they've received. These metrics should not be your only goal. The main concern should be ROI (return on investment). With the right tools and some knowledge, this can be calculated fairly easily.

These obstacles may seem overwhelming, but you don't have to worry about them. Third-party developers are working to simplify your Facebook marketing process. There are a few tools that you should familiarize yourself with. These tools help to overcome or completely avoid these obstacles. Some of the most useful ones are listed below.

Flow

Developed by Driftrock, this is a tool designed for developing well-optimized and targeted ads for Facebook as well as Instagram. It syncs with your existing e-commerce platform and helps you collect customer data, allowing you to focus more accurately on your existing customer base. You can focus on your existing customers and mailing lists, or you can find new people who have the same characteristics as your current customer base.

Google Analytics

This tool is mainly used to track web traffic. If you do not use it in conjunction with your Facebook marketing campaign, you're missing out on some good things. With this tool, you can obtain segmentation analysis of the data like conversions, custom reports, display charts, and scorecards to see the changes in the performance of the content. It also tracks the data related to all the users who have visited your website and any actions they performed on the website. This is an ideal tool for determining the profitability of investments and the effectiveness of your location.

Agorapulse

With this tool, you can link your accounts centrally on Facebook, Twitter, Instagram, LinkedIn, and any other social networks. You can plan and publish your posts, track your activity on these social media sites, interact with your customers, and even track your competition in the marketplace.

Social Bakers

This is a social analytics tool that works with all available social networking applications. It helps you to conduct competitive research and provides you with information about your target audience, your ROI, and other data in the form of customizable reports that can be tailored to your goals.

DrumUp

This is a combination of content marketing and social media tools that helps you find content that is considered appropriate and effective for

200

your audience. DrumUp sifts through tons of content available online and uses a complex algorithm for recommending stories and content that's most relevant to your audience. Essentially, it does all the heavy lifting when it comes to finding the ideal content. It is quite easy to use and you can quickly review and create as well as publish the posts to your social media account. It also provides different analytics like the engagement rate and media analytics to measure the effectiveness of the content you are using.

Likealyzer

With this tool, you can analyze the reach and effectiveness of your Facebook page. All you have to do is specify the URL of your page. This tool notifies you of any errors in your layout and the type of activity your site has received. This is a free application.

ShortStack

This tool is designed to make it easier to create advertising and host competitions using Facebook. The interface of this application is quite simple, and it has several tools that you can use to create a campaign that meets your needs.

All of these tools have their pros and cons, so the choice of tools depends on your goals and preferences. Most of them offer free trials or are available for free. Get started, experiment a bit, and you can focus on what suits you. If you can streamline your strategy, automate this process, and measure your ROI correctly, you can take full advantage of what Facebook has to offer.

Business Marketing Applications

There are several applications that every Facebook marketer needs to have to be more successful. These apps are not officially created by Facebook, but they are designed to help you create a corporate page on Facebook.

These applications are quite simple to use, and they help you to manage your site better. They help you with the content of your page and even with tracking the progress.

Custom tab applications

Tabs are available under the Facebook cover photo, and you can also find them in the Facebook Page tabs. These tabs are like the website navigation for your Facebook page that allows the users to browse through your page.

With custom tab applications, you can customize videos, pictures, and anything that's not on a tab. These applications are very useful because not everyone has excellent editing and computer skills. If you're one of those people, these applications will do anything for you so you can offer your customers everything they need. Recommendations: Hayo and Tabsite

Email capture apps

These apps allow you to track email addresses from your Facebook audience without causing them any disturbance. Gaining email addresses from people can be rather tricky at times. By obtaining the email addresses of your target and potential customers, you can ensure that you are keeping in touch with them and are providing them with interesting content that keeps them hooked on your business or brand. You can get an email address from people visiting your page and encourage them to click on specific links. This prevents you from having to request email addresses directly. Recommendations: Constant Contact and AWeber.

Applications for surveys and conducting polls

These are the applications that help conduct surveys and polls on your page. Polls and surveys are an important way to get customer feedback. The more reviews you have, the better you can serve your customers.

You can also gain valuable information. For example, are you curious about what your friends and followers think? What they like and don't like? Do you want to ask them about their opinions and want the results in an easy-to-understand format?

If yes, then you need to use poll and survey apps like Woobox, SurveyMonkey, and Antavo. This is one of the easiest ways to understand what your audience likes and dislikes. With the help of this data, you can create better-performing ads.

Automatic publishing applications

These are applications that can be a salvation for those who do not have the time to update their business page on Facebook regularly. Automatic publishing is available on Facebook, and here you can now create a message and then specify when this message should be displayed. The message automatically appears on your page at the specified time. This is very useful because not everyone has the time to publish materials on their site regularly. If you do not publish regularly, your page will gradually become less interesting. If this happens, you will not only lose your existing followers, but it will become rather difficult to attract new followers too. Scheduled publishing will ensure that your page appears active, even if you're too busy to publish. This can be done directly on Facebook or in applications that do this for you.

Recommendations: Buffer and Rignite.

Social integration applications

When integrated into social networks, different social network sites can be used with just one application. With these applications, you can connect various social networking sites to your Facebook page so that everything you post on other social networking sites will also appear on your Facebook page. For example, when you post on Twitter or Instagram, that content will automatically be placed on your Facebook page using social integration apps. Your audience will benefit the most from this, as many users only follow a few social networking sites. These users can easily contact you on other social networking sites when they see your Facebook posts.

Recommendations: Pagemodo and Tabsite.

Competitive applications

With competitor apps, you can organize competitions on your Facebook page to increase your participation in the company and engage your audience. Competitions can be difficult to organize and require a lot of effort; you even need to review the terms that Facebook has set for organizing competitions. You can do this with contest apps because they help you organize a contest and make sure you follow Facebook's terms. Recommendations: Offerpop and Votigo.

Chapter Three
Develop a Facebook Marketing Strategy

Develop a Strategy

The growth of Facebook will not slow down, and its popularity only continues to grow. Marketing on Facebook has grown and become its own new marketing tactic that requires a separate knowledge base than other types of advertising. So, if you want to start marketing on Facebook, you need a strategy. In this chapter, you will learn how to develop a marketing strategy for your company on Facebook.

Your goals

In life, without concrete goals, no strategy can be formulated. The same applies to Facebook marketing.

Goals help you identify the actual marketing needs of your business. If you want to use Facebook for marketing purposes or to improve an existing strategy, you have some needs in mind.

Do not set unrealistic goals that depend on indicators such as the number of likes or the number of subscribers. Instead, you have to solve your basic problems. For the company, some goals will be to improve the quality of sales, increase value in the organization, increase the pulse in the industry, and improve growth. Facebook can help to achieve these goals.

The first step to improve sales quality will be to improve your orientation. If you follow a sophisticated marketing strategy on Facebook, you can reach your target group very effectively.

Do not assume that the bigger the pond, the more fish you catch. You have to understand that Facebook is just a means by which you can achieve your goals. With Facebook, you can build relationships with your customers, build awareness, and deliver the best resources to your audience.

Reflect on your business model. Do you feel that your competitors are always one step ahead of you? Well, you can create a variety of social media monitoring tools to track the movement of your competitors in the marketplace.

Social recruiting is not easy, but it is certainly a popular technique nowadays. Social networks, especially Facebook, can be used to facilitate the recruitment process. More sensible growth means an increase in acquisitions, a reduction in churn, and a reduction in costs. Well, Facebook can help achieve this. Facebook helps lower advertising costs, increase targeting, and improve sales on social networks. These elements are incorporated into Facebook's marketing strategy and can help you achieve the organizational goals you may have set.

By marketing on Facebook, you can achieve these goals with less effort than traditional methods. The point is to work smarter, not harder.

Facebook demography study

Demographics are an important element of any marketing strategy, and marketing on Facebook is no different. If you use the extensive Facebook network, you'll find that more than 1.6 billion registered users see their news feeds every day. Therefore, it is very important to find out how to contact them. In addition, it is very important to know the latest demographic data of the users as these numbers are constantly changing.

Age and gender are not an obstacle to the use of Facebook. Anyone with an Internet connection and a smartphone can create a profile on this network. Facebook is no longer limited to the younger generation. Do not make the mistake of thinking that only 18- to 25-year-olds are active on Facebook. Facebook demographics are spread all over the world. The versatility is so great that if it represents a business; try to make the most of it. Your company has access to an international portal that transcends physical boundaries. This is the best platform for implementing a marketing strategy aimed at your audience, regardless of their location.

Choose and plan your content on Facebook

Every social networking platform has its content style, and Facebook is quite versatile. Your brand has a variety of content strategies to choose from, and it is possible to view Facebook stories, live streams, pictures, videos, or just content. Truly, the possibilities the platform has to offer are endless. However, keep in mind that it's all about the quality of the content being published with the audience and the expectations you place on your Facebook page.

Remember that you should actively promote your business, but do not go beyond your Facebook page and act like a used car dealership with many aggressive salespeople. The content you want to publish should be informative, interesting, and compelling. It has to have value for the audience. Your Facebook page should promote, but not be limited to, advertising. You need to highlight the values of your brand, identify your audience, and create a space that is completely unique and specific to your business or brand.

Once you understand the importance of the content, you must find a content form that suits you. Let's take a look at the different types of content that you can choose from and how you can best use them.

Status

This is probably the simplest form of communication available on this platform. When used correctly, it can also be very effective. By adding several new features that allow you to resize text and select the background color, you can highlight the status and make it more attractive.

Pictures

Posts with pictures are more effective when it comes to the degree of participation. Do not rely on pictures to do all the work for you. You must use high-quality images that will surprise your audience. It should be tasteful, creative, and attractive. Only in this way can you attract the attention of your audience.

Video

Video is in high demand these days. When posting videos, know that few users watch the video with sound as it should be viewed. The best-posted videos are not too long, are easy to understand, and always have a caption. The video should not make the user feel like watching it was a waste of time.

Links

This is an ideal tool for sharing news related to the industry and your business. You need to find interesting content and then share links to such content. This is a great way to engage your audience without having to create your own long posts.

Facebook Live

This method gets the most attention on Facebook. As your current content grows, your brand or business can interact with the world and your audience in real time. If there is a product launch, you can live with it! This will help attract the attention of a broad audience.

Facebook Stories

If you're using Snapchat, you should be up to date on Snapchat news. Similarly, Facebook developed the story of Facebook. Your Facebook history may consist of small clips that the user can view at any time.

The types of content you can post are vast, and once you've determined what content you want to use, you'll need to set a time to publish that content. The last thing you want to do is publish random content just to post something. Content planning means thinking about it before publishing. This ensures that the published content is of high quality. It also increases the chances that your company attracts an audience. However, sometimes, you may not have time to create content. In that case, you can use social media publishing tools like Sprout Social to develop content for your Facebook page. Do not hurry to schedule the release, take a moment to review the content, then decide when to publish it.

Find out Your Advertising Strategy on Facebook

Your Facebook advertising strategy should be such that it promotes awareness of your brand. When developing an advertising campaign on Facebook, you need to consider two things: cost-effectiveness and relevance. It's important to stay within the budget allocated for marketing. Budget is important if you want to avoid unnecessary clicks or overexposures. If you do not spend your money wisely, it can easily affect the goal of social media marketing.

The Facebook ads you use should also be relevant. To address a broad audience is not necessarily a bad thing. However, what may be relevant for one group may not apply to another. If you know your audience, you can create ads according to their needs. This prevents you from developing content that will only appeal to a small portion of your audience.

Start chatting and do not wait for your audience to take the first step

You must remember that Facebook is a social networking platform. The basis of such a platform is communication and interaction. Therefore, communicate with your audience and do not wait for your audience to take the first step. If you are passive in this aspect, it will discourage your audience from interacting with you, which will only hurt your business. Start interacting with your existing and potential customers. Keep them up to date with the latest information about your business without overwhelming them with information. Marketing on Facebook allows you to communicate with your customers and potential customers. So, make the most of it.

Encourage your entire workforce to use this platform

Facebook is a really good resource to protect the interests of employees. You can reach your audience by providing shared content to your employees. That way, you can also use your employees to increase your Facebook presence. This will help to increase the reach of your business.

Some marketers struggle with finding content that their employees would be willing to share. And some employees are either too eager or too scared to share corporate content on social networks.

You should start with a Worker Protection Program that empowers your employees to use truly large networks, such as Facebook, to share information about the company. Use Facebook as a promotional tool to showcase the various benefits of the company, new job opportunities, the work environment, and more. Use your staff and encourage them to promote your business on social networking platforms.

Track and analyze your marketing strategy

If you want your Facebook marketing strategy to succeed, you should make sure that it's analyzed regularly. There are various advertising measurements that you can use for this purpose.

If you want to make changes to or improve your strategy, you'll get useful information from the Facebook analytics tools. Every social media marketer should know about these tools. There are several free and paid applications that you can use to evaluate the effectiveness of your strategy.

You need to understand what works and what does not work to develop a strategy that is the most effective. This is where Facebook Insights comes into play. This will help you to understand what strategy works, what content attracts your audience, what likes and preferences your audience has, and other important data.

As you develop a marketing strategy for Facebook, your business can take full advantage of this platform.

Facebook Marketing: Things to Consider

Now that you are aware of the different steps to follow to create a Facebook marketing strategy, there are certain things you must consider while doing so.

Leverage the traffic

Remember, it is always a good idea for a business to have a website since it helps act as your storefront or even as the hub for all sales transactions. Your website will be the place where people can learn more about your business or even purchase the products or services you offer.

A good way to start marketing is by using the existing traffic on your website by including icons for social media which are easily visible. You can place certain direct links to your business's Facebook page or any other social media networking site on your website.

Most websites tend to place social media icons on either their homepage or the header because of the visibility these two places offer. It, in turn, helps create a better click-through rate or CTR placement.

Using your email signature

If you are currently using email as a means to stay in touch or contact your customers, then you must try to make the most of your email signature. You must start including your business page URL in your email signature. Including the URL to your social media pages in the email signature or the email messages ensures the recipient sees the link.

The chances of the viewer clicking on the link also increase. This, in turn, helps convert the recipient into potential leads or even increase the traffic to your social media pages. If you have any upcoming events on your Facebook page, then you must include the details about the same in your email signature in the form of a call-to-action button or a direct link to the concerned event.

Email blast

Before you can think about marketing on Facebook, your first step must be to ensure others are aware of your Facebook presence. You can send an email blast to ensure this. You can use any email service of your choice like MailChimp, AWeber, or any other service you like.

The best days of the week to send out an email blast are between Monday and Wednesday. Try to avoid sending out such emails during the weekends because a lot of users don't access their email accounts over the weekend.

In-store promotions

If you have a physical storefront, then you must consider in-store promotions.

Do your customers visit your store? If yes, then you can start informing your customers about your brand or business's presence on Facebook and other social media sites when they visit your store. If you have a physical storefront, then online marketing is as important as offline marketing. You can include the details about your social media pages on your business cards, on the packaging you use, on mirrors and doors at the store, or any other easy-to-notice place in the store.

The ideal day to post

An incredibly important feature of Facebook is the Insights. By going through your Posts Insights, you can easily determine the time where most of your target audience is online. If you want to schedule three posts per week, you must check the time where most of your followers are online and select those hours to post the content you want.

To access the Posts Insights, you must go to your Facebook Page and click on See Insights and open the Posts option. Now you can schedule the day on which you want to post, and you can also select the ideal time for the post. There are different third-party tools you can use to measure the metrics you need, like Hootsuite or Sprout Social.

Status updates

Facebook has hundreds of millions of users every day. Those millions of daily users can include your potential customers too.

If you want to use Facebook optimally, then you must post content which will appeal to your target audience. Your goal must be to post content which will satisfy at least one of these criteria: entertainment, education, or empowerment.

There are a couple of things you must keep in mind while posting status updates. Try to include the relevant emoticons to make the posts seem inviting. Including questions in your posts will increase the comments you receive.

If you don't think you will be able to post your status updates at a specific time every week, then you can start using Facebook's built-in feature, which allows you to schedule your posts.

Facebook plugins

If you want to work on improving your brand awareness, increasing your followers, and branding, then you must include Facebook plugins on your business website. You can include plugins for your official blogs too. There are different plugins you can use like Facebook Like Box or the Like Button. So, experiment with a couple of plugins until you find something that works well for you.

Chapter Four
Components of Facebook Marketing

Regardless of the size of the company, Facebook is now part of the marketing strategy of most businesses. Although popular and used by many, many marketers fail to fully utilize all the features Facebook offers to create brilliant marketing campaigns. This means that both entrepreneurs and marketers need to understand the different strategies and methods that contribute to creating a positive ROI, or return on investment. This chapter describes the different components of marketing on Facebook and the practical steps to implement them. The main components of marketing on Facebook are:

- Facebook page optimization

- Facebook groups

- Social sharing on Facebook

- Visibility of your posts

- When and how often to send

- Paid options

- Best practices for advertising on Facebook

Facebook Page Optimization

Your Facebook page is the starting point for all your Facebook marketing efforts. It would be ideal if it were evaluated on both Google and Facebook so your customers and potential customers can easily find your brand. Once they have found your page, people should like the page. Here are some things you can do to optimize your site for the purposes mentioned above:

Choose a username that is meaningful and memorable

This type of URL is called a vanity URL. The web address of your Facebook page is your username for your Facebook page (e.g., www.facebook.com/name of your company). Each page is assigned a default URL consisting of numbers. Your username should be such that it reflects the topic of your page or the name of your entire company so that search engines and customers can easily find your business in Google and Facebook searches. You need at least 25 likes if you want this URL.

Use descriptive keywords in the "About" section

The About section on your Facebook page is considered the primary source of textual property you own. Make sure the description of your business and products is as accurate as possible and use keywords that users can use when searching for their questions. While selecting the keywords, ensure that you go through other Facebook pages similar to yours and pick some keywords from there. Ask yourself, if someone had to search for your business or brand online, what are the words they would likely associate with your brand? Make a list of such words and keep it handy.

You should also always include the URL of your website in the description you provide. This will encourage users to click on it.

Use the appropriate category for your business

Most often, companies and businesses tend to choose the wrong category. In this way, they reduce the likelihood of being displayed in the Facebook chat search. If you're a local business, you need to make sure you pick the right category for your business. There are different categories to choose from like celebrities, bands, artists, local business, company, organization, charity or a community, but try to pick the one that most accurately describes you and your business or brand.

Optimize the images on your page

The first thing people see when they visit your site is your cover image and profile photo. The images you use should be of good quality and reflect what your brand wants to emit. The images used must be of reasonable size. This means that the photo on the cover should be about 851 x 315 pixels in size, and the profile image should have a size of 160 x 1160 pixels. Avoid grainy or poor-quality images. The images you use must also be relevant to your brand or business and should not be random. For example, if you are a local restaurateur, then posting images about the latest developments in the automobile industry doesn't make any sense.

Pinned posts

No matter what you think, most users only visit your page once. They are interacting with your page through the news displayed in their newsfeed, but they don't usually open your business page over and over again.

For this reason, the main function of your page is to convince the user to click the Like button. Facebook allows the page administrator to attach a message to the top of the page. Make sure that the topic of this post, which can be attached, is interesting and unique and attracts the attention of the page visitor.

Use Facebook Groups

The main tool that all businesses on Facebook should use to market their business is a Facebook page. But even groups can be an effective marketing strategy in different industries and niches. When used properly, groups can help generate a lot of traffic and even increase your business engagement. By participating in other industry groups, you can establish yourself as an authority in your field. Providing useful tips and useful information will help you become a valuable member of a group, and once people trust you, they will want to learn more about you and your business.

One of the most important uses of the Facebook group may be to create and participate in groups that are within your area of interest. Groups allow you to interact personally with your audience. It will also help your company to engage in regular discussions with your target audience.

Create a group that is responsive to anything that has to do with your niche or industry. For example, if you were a contractor, it would be a good idea to set up a group on Facebook where people can ask questions or discuss repairs, construction projects, and more. You can include all other users who you think will be able to contribute to the group or might at least help with your promotional efforts.

Promote Social Sharing on Facebook

Your corporate website and Facebook need to work together. Your sales funnel, or the journey a potential customer goes on when deciding to make a purchase helps direct the traffic from your Facebook page to your blog or website.

However, you also need to make sure that you give visitors to your site the ability to like and share the pages on Facebook, as well as to interact with your site. Make sure all content on your site has a Like and Share button that appears right next to it. These buttons can be added manually, or you can use various third-party services like AddThis or even the WordPress plugin to customize your buttons and make adding them to your website easier. You can also add something like "View posts" to give your site visitors a preview of the type of content that is typically posted on your social media pages.

Increase the Visibility of Your Posts

A common complaint that the majority of site owners share is that most of their fans have not seen their posts on Facebook. Facebook successfully studied this problem, and they managed to narrow the problem down to two main factors.

The first is the amount of content published on Facebook. This means that the user's newsfeed does not have enough space to display each message. The competition for publishing and appearing in the user's newsfeed is very stiff, and this results in a reduction of the impact on regular posts.

The second reason for limiting the visibility of the post is that the Facebook algorithm has been designed to display only the content most relevant to its users. Relevance is now determined by many factors, including the way a person interacted with a page in the past, the type of posts published, and the popularity of previous posts on the page among its users. Simply put, the more popular your posts are, the more visible they are. The following two tips can improve the visibility of your posts in the fan feed.

- Using video in your publishing strategy. Videos are more attractive and can help attract the viewer's attention.

- Look at the Insights page to determine the type of content that appeals to your audience. Page Insights typically contain a lot of content-type data that can help you interact more with your audience. Find out about the formats of the messages that are most visible (images, videos, links, or lyrics) and topics that appeal to your audience. Also, keep track of the days and times, as well as the frequency of publishing, that seem to work very well with your audience.

To get the most out of your advertising, you need to make sure the content you provide is attractive. Yes, you can use Facebook to publicize your business, but this is also an opportunity to create and maintain lasting relationships with your target audience. Ask yourself, "Will my fans find this article interesting for reading and interacting, even if they are not interested in buying a product I offer?"

When and How Often to Send

Some business owners focus on publishing at the right time and on the right day to ensure optimal coverage and interaction. However, the truth is that there is no fixed approach to publishing that meets the needs of all users. Online research may be available on this topic. However, please do your research. Be sure to consult Facebook Insights to make sure these methods fit your target audience.

Some people tend to believe that posting on Thursdays and Fridays results in a higher level of participation, and others believe that posting between noon and 3:00 pm helps maximize visibility. You can test these two theories yourself with Facebook Insights.

When it comes to the frequency of publication, you need to understand that there is a difference in being informative and annoying. Spamming your page with multiple posts will discourage your audience from following you. Some companies have managed to publish 5 to 10 times a day, and some may publish 1 to 3 messages a week, and they find that this is also effective.

SocialBaker, an artificial intelligence-backed social media marketing company, has found that posting less than two posts a week does not help attract your audience, and you may even lose interaction with them. If you publish more than two posts per day, you bombard your audience with too much information. Therefore, the ideal number of posts you should publish per week should be between 5 and 10. This will help to ensure maximum engagement.

Use Paid Options

It is quite possible to use free strategies to achieve decent visibility for your messages. But you should strongly consider looking for ways to supplement these organic strategies with some paid ones.

Currently, Facebook has two ways to increase the reach of your posts. The first one is by boosting the post. That way, you can improve the visibility of your message in your user's news feed. You can choose to have your message appear to subscribers to your page, your fans' friends, or other users you select. The targeting options available to your message include your interests, age, gender, and location of your ideal audience. To improve a specific post, you must click "Boost" when creating a new post. You'll also find this option in old posts if you want to extend an already published post. Improving the quality of posts is a very simple and effective way to increase the reach of your posts.

The second way to use paid options is to promote posts. They can be accessed through the Facebook Ad Manager. To create your advertised listing, you'll need to open the Facebook Ad Creator and click on the "Enlarge" option for your posts. Even though this is called a "promotion," the targeting and budgeting parameters can be better customized than just the "promotion" option on the page. You will learn more about Facebook Ads in the subsequent chapters.

When Should a Specific Post be Advertised?

One of the main difficulties for business owners or marketers on Facebook is to understand when to promote a post. In general, you want to promote news that helps you achieve a specific goal, such as increasing traffic to your website or promoting the sale of a particular product. Once you have chosen the position you want to advertise, consider the STIR strategy. With this strategy, you can answer specific questions before you publish a post. STIR is the acronym for a strategy known as Shelf life, Timing, Impact, and Results, which are the questions you should ask yourself when considering promoting a post. Once you analyze the content according to the specific aspects of the STIR strategy, you will be able to decide whether you must promote such content or not.

Facebook Ads

Facebook offers various advertising options. You can choose the ad type based on different goals. As mentioned earlier, one of these goals may be to increase or promote a particular item. However, there are several options, such as promoting your page, sending others to your website, increasing conversion rates, and requesting offers from users.

After selecting your campaign goal, you can select the targeting and budgeting options and select the ad you want to use for your ad. Choosing a destination for your campaign will help you achieve your advertising goals. There are three options: a newsfeed on the desktop, a mobile newsfeed, and a column on the right. The default option is that all these options are selected. You can select the placement of the ad according to your preferences.

Spending a lot of time and money on advertising on Facebook is a pretty easy way to achieve goals, and advertising is an effective way to get traffic, likes, and conversions. However, certain practices are very effective and can help you achieve your goals in a relatively simple way.

Always use audience targeting

Advertising for a broad audience without any orientation is a tedious task, and you are preparing for failure. Not only that, but it will also be a waste of time and money because you are not guaranteed to be successful or to appeal to a large number of people. There are many options for targeting, and one thing you should try is choosing the target audience based on their behavior.

The most important content should be placed first

Most users will probably only look at the content that was placed at the beginning of your ad. For this reason, it is very important that the content that you consider important is at the very top of your ad. This can be a link or a call to action.

Rotation of advertising

If you use specific targeting for your ad and, therefore, need to serve ads to a small audience repeatedly, this means that you must change the image used for your ad every one or two weeks. Reusing the same content will simply bore your customers, and it also reduces the chances of them following your page. It is very likely that your target audience will miss your ad.

Use conversion pixels to track the performance of your ads

If you want to buy multiple ads, you should use conversion pixels to identify ads that can help you reach your goals. Facebook Pixels helps you track conversion data. You can choose from a variety of conversion types when creating a pixel. This includes checks, registrations, generated page views, leads, etc. See the Facebook Help page for more information.

Use different ads for different placements

On Facebook, you can use the same images and copy them for different ads. It is very important that created ads are created for different platforms. The announcements displayed in the newsfeed on the phone, the desktop, and the right-hand column of the desktop differ significantly. These differences should be taken into account. The ads you create for a mobile app might not be optimized for viewing on the desktop and vice versa. So, while creating ads, please ensure they are optimized for different devices.

You can also use a call-to-action to specifically tell your users what you want them to do. This encourages the users to take the action you want them to. Facebook is an excellent platform to not only find your audience but also to interact with them. When used properly, you can increase traffic flow, visibility, and conversion rate.

Chapter Five
Using Facebook Marketing

Many social networking applications are available today. Facebook, however, is the reigning champion. This platform is much more than just a place for communication with people. In recent years, it has become a place where businesses can promote themselves and any products or services and interact with existing and potential customers. In this chapter, we take a look at the different ways to use Facebook for marketing. Regardless of the size of your business, Facebook is an excellent marketing tool.

Make the Most of the Business Page

A free marketing tool for businesses is your business's Facebook page. On this page, businesses and brands can not only post information about their products and services, but can also post links, images, and text. This page can be customized to help the target audience understand the persona of the business or brand. Your Facebook corporate page will help you develop your brand identity and allow you to show the human side of your business. You do not have to be formal when posting content on Facebook; you can loosen up your tie a little.

You have to consider what content your potential audience will see. You can post images on social networks, links, videos, etc. if this is relevant to your business and you think your audience appreciates it.

For example, if you own a local shoe store, maybe you can post videos of animals walking around in tiny shoes, or you may publish an article that will provide readers with information on how to measure the size of their feet and shoe type or inserts that help with pain in the legs and other benefits. The content you publish should be entertaining, educational, and content updates to your business.

Facebook has a personalized form of advertising in the form of Facebook Ads. They appear in the page columns of the Facebook site. They contain a title, a slogan, a picture, and a link that redirects the user to another Facebook page, a Facebook-linked application, or even an external website. By incorporating Facebook advertising into your Facebook marketing strategy, you can increase the number of likes or clicks on the site.

Advertising features on Facebook include demographic targeting (which uses user data based on their age, location, education, and interests). You can set advertising budgets and test ads (multiple versions can be tested simultaneously to compare their designs and settings), which are built-in tools to measure the effectiveness of advertising.

Facebook does not publish the click-through rate or the CTR data, so their overall effectiveness is unknown. Facebook ads have a click-through rate of 0.051%, and the average CPC (Cost per click) is about $ 0.80. However, these costs may vary depending on the targeting options and the competition. Once the user likes your page, they essentially become subscribers to your corporate page. All your messages and actions are displayed in their newsfeed. This will increase the number of users interacting with your business and help build relationships that can lead to conversions in the foreseeable future. You will learn more about the different costs involved later on in this book.

Facebook Contests

Another marketing tactic for Facebook that can help you increase your fan base and visibility is through contests or sweepstakes. If you are hosting a contest on Facebook, you should understand that these contests cannot be done through Facebook—as in, if you are hosting a contest where the winner will be decided based on the most number of likes or comments received on a specific post, it does get tedious to manually go through all the posts. Instead, using a third-party application is a good idea.

Most businesses use third-party applications to create a Facebook competition, and then they redirect users from the Facebook page to this application. There are several free and paid applications that you can use for it. Applications like ShortStack provide you with different competition templates, and Pagemodo is a free application for Facebook competitions.

An example of a simple Facebook contest idea is "like to win" content. If your business wants to increase its online visibility, then this is a good contest to conduct. The users merely need to like a specific post on your page to enter the contest, and the winner can be chosen through a lucky draw.

Facebook Sponsored Posts

Facebook page owners must pay a fee to ensure that their posts reach a certain number of users in order to increase their reach and impressions through the use of advertised Facebook messages.

Some may wonder why they have to pay for their subscribers to see their contribution. Well, if the user likes the page, the information and updates to this page should be displayed in their news feed, right?

The answer might not always be "yes." The above assumption only works if the user spends all of their time on the Facebook newsfeed. That does not happen often, does it? Who will spend all their time watching the news feed on Facebook?

Therefore, it is likely that the user will not see updates to your page in their news feed. If your subscriber views their newsfeed as and when your article is published, chances are the user will see your post. However, there is no guarantee that this will be done.

So, this is where the concept of sponsored posts comes in. Through a sponsored post, you can increase the chance of being seen in the user's newsfeed. Sponsored posts are visible to existing fans and can connect with fans' friends. Configuring the promoted messages is easy. Just click on the button that appears below the messages on your page.

Facebook Open Graph

Facebook Open Graph connects your Facebook page with other sites for your business. This allows companies to mark the actions of a particular user in their application. Billions of interactions are published daily with the Facebook Open Graph.

Businesses can create third-party applications that contact the user and send notifications to Facebook when that user performs a specific action with that application. This provides the opportunity for creative interaction options that go beyond the usual Like and Comment parameters. Messages can encourage users to listen, to try, to read, or to offer something creative that a business has to offer. In most cases, a website or application that prompts the user to log in to Facebook has something to do with the user's connection through the open Facebook graphic.

Spotify is an example of how Facebook Open Graph becomes an incredibly useful tool in Facebook marketing. It all starts with an invite to open Facebook. Normally, this is followed by a permission request, and most users usually click on it without thinking about it. Upon receiving user approval, Spotify may broadcast the songs the user hears in a friend's news feed. Spotify offers users various options, such as the favorite song that your friend listens to that you can now listen to or to even add it to your favorites in the Spotify app.

Open graphics options like these are unique and different from all the clutter that is usually present in the user's newsfeed. Most Facebook games typically use the Facebook Open Graph options when they post a notification, when a user unlocks a level, or when a user completes a level. This strategy seeks to leverage the concept of word-of-mouth marketing.

Sponsored Stories

This is a type of advertising on Facebook that shows user interactions with their friends. Sponsored Stories aims to maximize the use of word of mouth. For example, if a user sees their friends like this page, they are more likely to notice this page. The goal of Sponsored Posts is to make users do the same things as their friends. When a friend of a user likes a page or announces a proposal, information about it is published in the user's newsfeed. However, these messages are usually easily overlooked. With Sponsored Stories, you can ensure that these posts are in a preferred position and appear in the news feed and the right pane. For mobile devices, Sponsored Stories is the only ad format available.

Advertising stories are not just about likes or offers; they can also be used with all Facebook Open Graph applications. If a friend has Scramble with Friends installed on Facebook, Sponsored Stories show users their friend just played this game and invited them to "challenge them" or "play with them" or another similar option. They are more effective than regular Facebook ads. Use the Facebook ad creation flow to create ad stories on Facebook easily.

Share on Facebook

With Facebook, advertisers can maximize the retargeting of Facebook ads with real-time bidding. Advertisers can focus on their potential audience using data about the history of their web search. Each time a user visits a product page on a merchant's website but does not make a purchase, they can use FBX (Facebook Exchange) on Facebook to run an ad for the same product. Previously, Facebook ads with retargeting were shown in the sidebar, but these ads have been shown in the news feed these days. This is good news for all FBX advertisers as the speed of responses to ads in the newsfeed is higher than the number of ads placed in the right column.

Chapter Six
Facebook Pixel

If you want to use Facebook ads, there is one important tool you must start using immediately. The tool is called Facebook Pixel, and it can help you make the most of your social advertising budget. In this section, we will take a look at how using Facebook Pixel can benefit you and your business.

The Benefits of Facebook Pixel

What is Facebook Pixel? Facebook Pixel is a simple code which can be included on your website. It helps collect data that you can later use for optimizing ads, building a targeted audience for ads, tracking conversions from Facebook ads, and remarketing to those who have taken some action on your website in the past. Facebook Pixel helps track users who interact with your website or Facebook ads by using cookies. The Facebook conversion pixel and the custom audience pixel were initially the two types of pixels available. However, Facebook discontinued the conversion pixel in 2017, and if you were using it, then you need to switch over to the latest version of Facebook Pixel.

What do you need Facebook Pixel? It provides information that comes in handy while creating future ads on Facebook that better target your audience. The tracking data provided by Facebook Pixel helps make sure your target audience views your ads. It also tracks whether those people perform the action you desire. This, in turn, helps increase your rate of Facebook ad conversions and improves the ROI.

Uses of Facebook Pixel

Even if you haven't started using Facebook ads, you must install Facebook Pixel immediately. It will start collecting all the essential data right away, so you don't have to start from scratch when you are ready to create a Facebook ad.

Conversion tracking

Facebook Pixel enables you to see the way people interact with your website upon viewing your Facebook ad. You can also start to track customers across various devices. This essentially means you can see if users view your ads on a mobile device and switch to a desktop before taking the desired action (maybe making a purchase) or if it is the other way around. By keeping this data in mind, you can fine-tune your ad strategy and calculate your ROI.

Facebook retargeting

By using the data from Facebook Pixel, you can retarget and create dynamic ads that are aimed toward users who have visited your website in the past. For instance, you can retarget those users who added a specific product on their wish-list on your website or left it in their shopping cart. This is a part of psychological marketing where you increase the chances of a user performing the desired action by increasing the visibility of your Facebook ad. Repeatedly seeing your Facebook ad makes the viewer more likely to follow through on the desired action, such as purchasing a product.

Lookalike Audiences

By using the targeting data, you can develop a profile of a lookalike audience consisting of users who share similar interests, likes, and demographics with those users who have interacted with your website. You can essentially increase your base of potential customers by using this technique.

Optimizing Facebook Ads

By using the pixel data, you can optimize your Facebook ads for better conversion as well as value. The only conversion you can work on optimizing is linking clicks if you don't have a Facebook Pixel. With Pixel, you can optimize the ads for such conversions in sync with your business goals like email sign-ups or product purchases. By using this data, you can also optimize your ads based on the value. You can track data related to aspects such as who buys from your site and how much they spend. By using Facebook Pixel, you can target your ads toward those users who are likely to make high-value purchases.

Better access

If you want to use web conversion campaigns, customize audiences from your website, or create dynamic ads, then you need Facebook Pixel. You also need this tool to track different metrics like cost per conversion or cost per lead.

How to Use Facebook Pixel

Facebook Pixel can be used for collecting data related to two different types of events. The two types of events include the predefined set of standard events and custom events. What is an event? An event is a term used to define a specific action a visitor must take on your website like signing up for an email list or buying a product.

There are 17 predefined standard events according to Facebook Pixel that you can use, and they are as follows:

- Purchase- whenever someone purchases on your website.

- Lead- whenever a user signs up for a trial or identifies themselves as a lead on your website.

- Complete registration- as stated in the name, it refers to the action where a user registers themselves on your website.

- Adding payment information- whenever a user enters their payment information while making a purchase on your website.

- Adding to the cart- whenever a user adds a product to their shopping cart on your website.

- Adding to wish list- whenever a user adds a product to their wish list on your website.

- Initiating checkout- whenever a user starts the checkout process or initiates a purchase on your website.

- Search- whenever a user uses the search option to look for something specific on your website.

- View content- whenever a user lands on a particular page on your website.

- Contact- whenever a user contacts you or your business.

- Customize the product- whenever a user selects a specific

238

variation of a product like color or design.

- Donation- whenever a user makes a donation to a charity of your choosing or any other cause you mention.

- Finding location- whenever someone tries to find the location of your business.

- Schedule- whenever a user schedules an appointment with your business.

- Starting a trial- whenever a user signs up for a free trial for something specific you offer.

- Submitting application- whenever a user applies for a specific program, service, or product you offer as a credit card.

- Subscribing- whenever a user subscribes to a paid-for service or product.

You can also include more details to the set of standard events available by using parameters or extra code. These parameters help customize the standard events according to the type of currency, content, basket contents, or the value of a conversion event. For instance, you can use Facebook Pixel to track the number of views a particular category receives on your website instead of tracking the overall views. If you have a website selling pet supplies, you can use the Facebook Pixel to track the views received for different categories of pet supplies.

The next option available to you is creating a custom event instead of using the regular events. You need to use URL rules based on particular URL keywords or URLs while creating a custom event.

Steps to Create a Facebook Pixel

Now that you are aware of the different metrics you can track and the benefits of tracking them, it is time to create a Facebook Pixel and add it to your website.

Step one: Create a pixel

Open Facebook Events Manager and click on (☰) present on the top left-hand side of the screen. The click on Pixels.

Now, click on the button "Create a Pixel."

Name the pixel, enter the website's URL, and click "Create."

While selecting the pixel's name, remember that you can only create on a pixel per ad account while using Events Manager. The name must align with your overall business instead of a particular campaign. If you use the Facebook Business Manager, you can use more than one pixel per ad account.

Step two: Add the pixel code

If you want to start using the pixel to gather information from your website, you must add some code to your website. There are a couple of ways you can do this, and it essentially depends on the website service or platform you use.

If you are using Squarespace, Google Tag Manager, or any similar e-commerce platform, you can install pixel without altering your website code. If you work with a developer or anyone else who can help edit your website code, you must provide them all the details they need to install pixel into your website. If neither of these options is applicable to you, you must directly install the pixel code into your website. There are several steps you must follow.

Click on the "Manually Install the Code Yourself" option while setting up your pixel. Now you need to copy and paste the pixel code into the header code of the website you want to use it on. You need to post the pixel code between the first </head> tag and the second <head> tag. You must insert the code into all the pages of your website or into any specific template you opt to use.

You will notice an "Automatic Advanced Matching" option on your screen in the setup menu. By turning on this option, the pixel helps match the hashed customer data from your website to the users' respective profiles on Facebook. It allows you to track the conversions precisely and creates a wider custom audience.

Enter your website's URL and click on "Send Test Traffic" option to check whether the code has been installed properly or not. Once the Facebook Pixel starts to track, you must click "Continue."

Step three: Track events

You must select the events you want to track using the toggle buttons. You can either select from any of the present 17 events or create your own custom events. For every event you select, you must select whether to track on inline action or the page load.

Track event on page load: This helps track those actions that involve going to a different page like when the sign-up process is completed successfully or when a purchase is made.

Track event on inline action: This helps track actions taking place within a page instead of opening another page like when a user adds something to their wish list or their shopping cart on the website.

You can also set certain parameters for an event. For instance, you might want to track the purchases made over a specific dollar value. If you want to use Pixel for custom events, you must go to Facebook Events Manager, click on Custom Conversions, select Create Custom Conversions, and define the custom conversion event accordingly.

Step four: Confirm if the pixel is working

If you used the "Send Test Traffic" in the second step, then you have already check to confirm that the pixel is working properly. However, before you start to rely on the data generated by the pixel, you must check whether it is tracking the data properly or not. Open your Google Chrome browser and add the Facebook Pixel Helper extension to it. This option is only available for Google Chrome. So, if you use some other browser, you must first install Google Chrome to start using Pixel Helper.

Open the page where you have included the pixel. If the extension discovers the pixel, then the </> extension icon turns blue and a popup will show up displaying the pixels it finds on the given page. This popup will inform you whether the pixel is working as intended or not. If not, then an error message will show up, and you need to make the necessary changes.

Step five: Add a pixel notice to your site

If you don't want to violate Facebook's terms of use, then you must be sure to include a notice on your website informing the users that their data is being collected. This means that you must provide an unambiguous notice that you are using Facebook Pixel and that the users' information is being collected via cookies or any other means. You must also inform the users they have the option to opt out of their data being collected. You must carefully go through Facebook's Business

242

Tool Terms about the Special Provisions Concerning the Use of Facebook Pixels and SDKs.

Facebook Pixel Cookies

Facebook changed the way it uses cookies for tracking the Facebook Pixel data in October 2018. Users now have the option to use first-party and third-party cookies. You don't have to make any changes unless you wish to opt out of using first-party cookies. What does this mean? Essentially, it allows advertisers to continue to track data on browsers like Safari and Firefox. These two browsers have placed restrictions on using third-party cookies. Advertisers involved in fields involving comprehensive privacy legislation like finance and health sectors might need to opt out for compliance purposes.

Chapter Seven
Facebook Advertising

Using Facebook Ads Manager

Do you want to start a Facebook ad but aren't sure where to begin? That's a common feeling, which is why this entire chapter is dedicated to the process of creating an ad. However, before you can run an ad campaign on Facebook, you must learn about the Facebook Ads Manager. It's a great tool that you can't do without when growing your business.

Create an Account

The first step is to learn how to set up an account on the Ads Manager. To get started, you must log into your Facebook account, open the drop-down menu present on the upper right corner of your account, and click on the "Create Ads" option. This will open an account for you and will help you set up and run your ad campaign on Facebook.

Explore Ads Manager

Once you open the main menu in the Ads Manager, you can see different options: Plan, Measure & Report, Assets, Create & Manage, and Settings. Once you start using Ads Manager frequently, you will notice another section, the "Frequently Used" section, where you can easily find all the tools you regularly use. Below are all the tools you will become familiar with when using the Ads Manager:

Plan

The "Plan" section includes tools to help you understand your target audience and give you ideas for running Facebook ads. The Audience Insights tool in this section will help you find all the information you need about your target audience on Facebook. It also allows you to create a custom audience based on things such as user interests, gender, age group, location as well as the pages they like. According to the parameters you select, Facebook Ads Manager will give you the necessary information you will need.

For instance, you can discover helpful advertising ideas when you ask Facebook to provide data about those users who like your Facebook page. You must first input information in Audience Insights for the information you need about the users who like your page. Based on the parameters you select, Insights will display various tabs about those users.

The first tab of information is related to demographics. The graph produced in this section will provide information about the age and gender of all the users who like your page. The demographic data also provides information about users' professions, marital status, and qualifications. Using this information, you can create content that will appeal to them.

When you open the Page Likes option in the Insights report, you can see data that will come in handy while creating content for your target audience. For instance, within an ad campaign, you can create different ads which target the segments of your audience based on the pages that they like or follow. If you are aware of the kind of pages they like and what those pages offer, you can create ads that will appeal to your audience.

Check all the information displayed under various tabs apart from Demographics and Page Likes to learn more about your target audience.

For instance, you can discover data related to the users' location, level of engagement on Facebook, household income, and purchases. You can also use this to analyze your custom audience and their specific interests. For instance, if the users who like your page also like another page on Facebook and you wish to learn more about the particular page, then you can ask Audience Insights to provide you the data of that page by including it in your interests option.

Another tool in the Plan section is the Creative Hub. You can use this to create mockups of your ad and share it with others to get their feedback or any other ideas.

Frequently Used

As the name suggests, this section shows the four most frequently used tools. Think of it as a quick action LaunchPad. If you don't see a specific tool you want to use like the Audience Insights, then you must click on the "All Tools" option, and you will be able to see a list of all the tools available.

Create and Manage

In this section, you will find the tools you need for creating and managing ad campaigns on Facebook. The Business Manager tool will come in handy if you have an advertising team or are using more than one page. If you sign up for "Business Manager" then it lends structure as well as organization to your Ads Manager account. You cannot access this tool without signing up for it. The Ads Manager tool will help run the ad campaigns and also analyze the data from those campaigns.

You can use Facebook Pixel and download the customized reports from it for further analysis.

The Power Editor is a brilliant advertising tool that helps you create ad campaigns. When creating ads, this tool offers different advanced features and options like running an ad on a schedule set according to the time zones, controlling the placement of the ad, optimizing the ads to increase engagement rate or impressions, bulk uploading, and running unpublished posts.

The Page Posts tool helps you view all the posts on your page and the way the users are interacting with the content you post. Different options like Scheduled Posts, Ads Posts, and Published Posts are available in this tool. You can also view data about the reach of your post, the total clicks or engagement generated per post, the number of users who took action, and the date of publishing. If you want to direct the traffic to your app (provided you have one) to increase the downloads of the app, you can use the App Ads Helper.

Another interesting feature in the "Create & Manage" section is the Automated Rules. Use this option to establish certain rules for your ad campaigns. It also helps you automate alerts or perform a specific action when the rules you set are met. For instance, you can set the rule to automatically stop an ad if its CPC, or cost per conversion, exceeds $5. If according to the tool's estimates, the CPC of your ad increases beyond $5, then the ad will stop being published until you review it.

By doing this, you can forego the need to constantly check your daily ad budgets. While creating rules, you have different parameters to adjust like the application of the rule you set, the way you want to receive notifications, the automatic action to be taken when the rule is met, and the frequency of the application of the rule, and the different conditions to be met.

Measure and Report

If you want to analyze how your ad campaign is doing, then you need to access the Measure & Report section of the Ads Manager. You can access various tools in this section like Ads Reporting, Custom Conversions, and Analytics. The Ads Reporting tool helps generate a report for an ad you are running. If you want to analyze any previous ads, you can set the date or the time frame within which the ads were run.

By analyzing the ads you run, you can create better ads in the future. If you want to compare various campaigns and analyze the different metrics of key performance, then this tool comes in handy.

For instance, if the key performance metric you want to analyze the ads on is the click-through rate or the cost per conversion, you can use this tool. Facebook Pixel automatically tracks certain key metrics related to the actions different users take on your website like viewing the content. Having a custom Facebook Pixel conversion will help you track specific actions (you can define this action) the users take.

The Custom Conversions tool, as the name suggests, helps create custom conversions, and you can also view all the custom conversions you created in the past. Custom Conversions enables marketers to track as well as to optimize for conversions without having to add anything extra to the Facebook Pixel code on the site.

You can also check when you received the pixel data and the custom conversions that are active now. You can include 40 custom conversions per ad account. To create a new custom conversion for tracking the activity on your website, you must click on the "Create Custom Conversion" option and fill in the necessary information in the popup menu. While doing this, you need to include a URL in the rule for tracking the activity. Once you create the custom conversion, you can generate a custom conversion ad and then select the custom conversions you wish to track for determining the success of the ad.

For instance, if the users who register themselves on your website are directed to a Thank You page, then place the Thank You page's URL in the Rule tab. This will ensure that whenever a user registers themselves and is directed to the Thank You page, the pixel records the action and notifies Facebook about the genuine conversion. After you create a custom conversion, refresh the page to enable the custom conversion.

The Analytics tool will enable you to analyze the data generated from your page and Facebook Pixel. As you create ads and work with the pixel, Analytics is a rather helpful tool that will optimize your marketing efforts on Facebook.

Assets

Another option in the main menu of the Ads Manager is Assets. This option gives you quick and easy access to all the important assets you used for creating your ads, including the images you used, data from the Facebook Pixel and your target audience, and more. The different tools available in this section are Audience, Pixels, and Offline Events.

The Audience tool allows you to create a custom audience while designing the ad. This tool also comes in handy while establishing your target audience for any future ads. If you want, you can save an audience, and you can access this while creating other ads too. You can create three types of audiences according to Facebook, and they are a custom audience, lookalike audience, and saved audience.

Custom audience refers to the kind of audience you are targeting according to certain parameters of your choice. A lookalike audience refers to an audience who shares similarities with your custom audience. Once you use a specific audience for creating an ad, you can save that specific audience for future reference.

According to your ad campaign objective, you can select a specific type of audience. For instance, according to the user's engagement on your website, Facebook page, or app, you can create a custom audience. Once you select the kind of custom audience, Facebook will guide you through all the options available. For instance, if you want to create your custom audience according to their Facebook engagement, you can select the different types of engagement you want to consider.

You can target audiences according to different parameters like those who viewed your videos, the ones who engaged with your page, or those who clicked on an ad. Once you set an engagement option, you need to select the specific interactions you wish to target. This means you can narrow down the options for your custom audience by setting specific ways in which you can define the audience you wish to target like interactions related to your page.

The custom audience option allows you to target all those users with whom you have had some interaction in the past whereas the lookalike audience option allows you to find other users who share attributes similar to the ones of your existing audience.

Once you select the lookalike audience option, click on the Source option to guide Facebook about the specific attributes you are looking for in users. After you do this, you must define two parameters, and they are the location of the audience and the audience size.

The Images option allows you to see the images you used in a recent ad or anything you might have picked up from other posts. The list of images displayed is sorted according to their recent use. The pixel option allows you to insert a Facebook Pixel or see the data obtained from any pixels you used in the past. You can use the pixel data to create better ads. For instance, if you notice that a specific post obtained a lot of views, then you can create an ad targeting those users who read the post and provide them a content upgrade if they provide their email address. It is a simple means of increasing your email list.

An Offline Event is a tool which helps you track all the activity that takes place outside Facebook. For instance, if someone who saw your ad on Facebook visits your physical store to make a purchase, this information will be included in this tool. If you want to create an offline event, you must input the customer data and compare it against all those who viewed your online ad.

The Settings tool is where all your basic account information is stored like payment information, email address, and any other particulars related to your account.

Chapter Eight
Setting up Facebook Ad Campaign

Setting up a Facebook Ad

Now that you understand the tools to use when creating a Facebook ad, it's time to examine how to actually create the ad.

Step one: Setting goals

Before you can start churning out ads, there is one step you cannot afford to skip: determining the goals for your Facebook ads.

Why do you want to advertise? What do you want the ads to achieve?

By establishing a couple of goals before creating your ads, you give yourself a yardstick for measuring your success. For instance, if you want to increase the number of downloads for an application you created by marketing it on Facebook via ads, then your goal can be something as simple as achieving 100 downloads within four weeks.

Here are some examples of potential goals you can set for yourself:

- Increasing the traffic to your website via Facebook ads

- Increasing your reach

- Improving the engagement rate of your Facebook page

- Increasing awareness about your brand

- Increasing purchases of a certain product

Step two: Facebook Ads Manager

Any ad campaign you want to run on Facebook must be supported by Facebook Ads Manager. You can access it from your Facebook account by selecting the "Manage Ads" option from the drop-down menu. Once you enter the Ads Manager, you can go through the different tools discussed in the previous section. To start creating your ad, you need to click on the green button located on the top right-hand corner of your Ads Manager page.

Step three: Selecting your objective

Now that you have opened the Ads Manager and are ready to create a Facebook ad, you must establish your marketing objective. You will find 15 options displayed on the pop-up window on your screen. The three main categories you need to set marketing objectives for are awareness, conversion, and consideration. Go through the different options available and select those that are in sync with the marketing goals you established in the first step.

The different objectives available under the category of "Awareness" are increasing your reach, increasing brand awareness, reaching those users near your business, promoting your page, and boosting your posts. If your marketing budget is rather limited, then the best way to go about marketing is by focusing on creating ads for awareness.

The different objectives available under the category of "Consideration" are collecting leads, getting video views, increasing the number of downloads of your app, increasing the attendance for any event, and directing the traffic to a landing page.

The different objectives under the "Conversion" category include increasing the rate of conversion on your website, encouraging users to claim any offers, promoting a specific product or catalog, increasing your rate of engagement for your app, and increasing the number of visitors to your physical store.

Once you select your marketing objectives, the next step is to name your marketing campaign.

Sep four: Budget and audience

There are two things you must do during the step: define your target audience and establish the ad budget. Customizing your target audience is critical. Regardless of how wonderful your ad campaign is, it will not generate the results you expect if it is not directed toward your target audience. You can customize your target audience according to different demographics such as location, age, gender, languages, interests, behaviors, and connections.

Once you select your target audience, you must concentrate on establishing the ad budget. When you are setting the ad budget, you must keep in mind that the amount you set represents the maximum limit you want to spend on the ad. The budget you want to set can be a lifetime budget or a daily budget. The daily budget refers to the average cost you will incur on the ad per day. The lifetime budget refers to the maximum amount of money you will spend during the lifetime of the ad.

Step five: Creating the ad

This is where the fun begins. You can select the images or the video, the header, the text, and the location for the displaying your Facebook ad. The text you want to include in the ad must not exceed 90 characters and will appear in the form of a quick message above the images or video in the ad.

There are two options you can use while creating ads on Facebook. The first option is to use an existing post, and the second option is to create a new option. You must consider which of these options meets your requirements before you decide to choose.

For certain ads, as with boosting posts, you can create the ad by using an existing post which was already published on your Facebook page. If you want to do this, you must click on the "Use Existing Post" option from the dashboard available on Facebook Ads Manager.

The other option you can go with is to create a new advertisement from scratch. Before you can start working on the creative elements, you must decide the format of the Facebook ad. There are five formats you can use for creating Facebook ads, and they are a carousel, single image, canvas, single video, and slideshow. A carousel ad includes two or more images or videos the viewer can scroll through. A single image ad is, as the name suggests, an ad based on one image, and you can create six variations of an ad using a single image. If you want the ad to include just one video, then the ad format you must opt for is a single video ad. A canvas format enables you to tell a story through an amalgamation of images and videos. The slideshow format helps loop video ads using up to 10 images.

The objective that you established in step three will determine the different ad formats available to you.

Once you have chosen an ad format, you must add content to the ad. This is a critical step and whether your ad will stand out or not depends on the content you include. If you want your ad to be successful, you must include appealing and enticing images, videos, or text, or a combination of all these three things. There are certain specifications given by Facebook for the images or videos you want to include in the ads.

The image specs recommended by Facebook are as follows: the image ratio must be 1.91: 1 and the image size must be 1200 X 628 pixels. To improve the effectiveness of the ad, you must avoid using images with text overlay on them. Facebook recommends that the videos you use for ads be in .MOV or .MP4 files format with a resolution of at least 720 pixels. The file size must not exceed 4 GB, the ideal video ratio must be 16:9, it must be at least one second long, and the maximum duration of the Facebook ad cannot exceed 240 minutes. Sound and subtitles are recommended but optional.

Step six: Selecting the ad placement

The ad placement refers to where you want the ad to be shown. Your ads can appear in the desktop News Feed, in the Facebook app News Feed, and the right-hand column. You also have the option of the ad appearing on Instagram. Facebook will recommend that you opt for the default placements based on the objective of your ad. When you select this option, Facebook's algorithm will automatically optimize the placement of the ads to generate the best results. However, you do have the option of selecting the placement based on what you want.

Step seven: Placing the order

Now, your ad is ready, and you must click on the "Place Order" option. Once the ad is submitted, Facebook will review it before it goes live. You will also receive a confirmation, usually an email, about the ad. Remember to make sure your ad meets Facebook's requirements as discussed in previous chapters.

Optimizing the Ad Budget

Now that you are aware of how to create an ad, you must also understand how to budget the ad. Are you struggling to decide how to structure your marketing budget for producing Facebook ads? Well, you will learn everything about optimizing the Facebook Ads budget in this section. Simply put, it all boils down to basic mathematics, and it isn't complicated. Once you carefully go through the information in this section, you will be able to establish a clear Facebook ad budget. Here is a quick overview of the different steps included:

- Establishing your campaign goals,

- Taking the time to work backward,

- Calculating your ideal size of the audience,

- Estimating the target impression count,

- Estimating your CPM,

- Calculating the cost per ad set and

- Combining all your ad sets to establish your overall ad campaign budget.

The first step is to state your goals. This step is essential when trying to set up a budget for your ads. When your goals are tangible, you can easily determine the costs involved in attaining those goals. The goals for your ad campaigns can be increasing the following areas: your product sales for a given period, the number of leads produced, the engagement rate on posts, RSVPs for events, user responses to a specific offer, video views, and the number of new followers acquired during the campaign. These are merely examples of the goals, and you can go through step one in the previous section to determine what goals to set.

To make things easier for the sake of explanation, we will consider a hypothetical situation throughout the next steps to understand how you can calculate the budget for a Facebook Ads campaign.

258

Now, you need to start working backward. This means you must start at the bottom and make your way up the conversion sequence.

Let us assume that you want your ad campaign to generate 300 product sales. Ask yourself, what comes before you close a sale? You will need to generate leads. If the rate of conversion is around 30%, then you will need to generate at least 1,000 leads to attain your goal of 300 sales. When it comes to Facebook leads, it essentially refers to your list of email subscribers. To produce leads, you must include the link to a specific landing page in your ad that will encourage the users to sign up for your email list. There are different ways in which you can generate leads (email subscription list), like offering a free eBook or an analytical report in exchange for a user's email address. However, your work doesn't end here. Essentially, you will need to work backward until you arrive at the top of your Facebook marketing funnel.

Here is a simple way to go about working this process: Relevant Facebook users > Followers > Leads > Customers. This is the path of how customers can be obtained.

As you start working backward, you will find that you may end up with a couple of different ad campaigns. You can use the "Page Like" campaign for converting your target Facebook users into the followers of your page. To convert followers into leads, you can use a list-building ad campaign. To convert your leads into customers, you need a website conversion campaign. That's three different campaigns to achieve the one goal of generating 300 sales.

After this, you must calculate the size of your ideal audience. In the previous step, we assumed that the goal of your ad campaign was to generate 300 sales. According to the rate of conversion of 30%, you need about 1,000 leads. So, what must the size of your target audience be on Facebook to generate 1,000 leads? There are various variables involved here. Consider the following: How many users will view your ads? How many of your targeted Facebook users will be active on Facebook daily?

What if your targeted users don't view the ad event after the Facebook ad is live?

Since you have no control over the number of times Facebook will display your ad to your targeted audience, what will be an ideal ad frequency to attain your goal? This is where you must set some limits and estimations. Some questions you must answer in this regard are: What is the duration of your ad campaign? How likely will your targeted audience be on Facebook during your ad campaign? How likely is it for Facebook to display your ad to your targeted audience?

So, do you plan on running the ad campaign for a week, two weeks, a month, or maybe six months? It is essential that you don't consider the entire duration of your overall marketing campaign. Instead, you must concentrate on how long you want to run this specific (ad) aspect of the campaign. Once you know the duration of the ad, you need to figure out whether your leads will be active on Facebook at least once during the length of the ad campaign. To determine the activity of your target audience on Facebook, you can monitor the data you gather from Facebook Analytics or even the Facebook pixel. The final question you must answer is whether or not Facebook will display the ad to your target audience while they are online. The higher the likelihood of your target audience viewing your ad, the lower your ad budget will be.

So, to go ahead with the previous illustration, let us assume that the ad campaign is being run for three months, the chances of the target audience being online during the length of the campaign is about 99%, and the likelihood of Facebook displaying the ads to your target audience while they are active online is 100%. So, if these are the numbers, will you be able to generate 1,000 leads? The answer is that you very well might be able to given the fact that you are running the campaign for three months. If you use basic math, then you must be gaining at least 10 more leads to cover the 1% loss in views. It means 1,000 leads divided by 99% gives you 1,010 leads. Usually, for a shorter campaign, you will need more leads.

Now, you will need to calculate the target impression count. To do this, you must use the ad frequency. This refers to the average ad frequency within the length of your campaign. You can optimize the ad campaign for post engagement, the CPC, impressions, and unique daily reach. When you select the option of unique daily reach, it allows you to limit the ad frequency to 1. So, to estimate your budget, you must estimate the average frequency.

To continue the example, let us assume that for a 3-month long ad campaign, you must aim for an ad frequency between 10 and 15 users per lead. So, for an audience size to generate 1,000 leads, and with the estimation of ad frequency between 10-15 for three months, you will have to aim to achieve an overall impression count of anywhere between 10,000 and 15,000 leads (multiply the number of leads you want to generate with the ad frequency).

The next step is to estimate the CPM, CPI, or the cost per impression. You need to figure out how much the ad impressions will cost you. CPMs usually differ according to the industry you belong to and your objectives. For instance, if you aim to run a campaign for website conversions, then a $10 CPM is a good starting point. To calculate the total cost of your ad budget, you must multiply the total impressions you want with the average cost of impression and divide it by 1,000.

So, (total impressions X CPM)/ 1,000 = total cost.

The final step is to calculate the cost per ad set. Now you have to follow the formula mentioned above. Using the formula, your cost per ad set will be: (1,000 impressions X $10)/1,000 = $100. It essentially means you need about $100 to convert 1,000 leads into 300 potential sales over three months.

Chapter Nine
Facebook Analytics

Facebook Analytics

If you want to make the most of all the analytical data provided by Facebook, then you must start using Facebook Analytics. Facebook Analytics is a brilliant tool that enables marketers to understand the journey of a targeted user across different Facebook channels and their path through the sales funnel or the path the customer takes toward purchasing the product.

This is a free tool and is designed to optimize the working of Facebook ads. According to the previous algorithms of Facebook, Facebook only allowed you to view the last touch point in the sales funnel. For instance, if a user interacted with six of your Facebook posts but only made a purchase on the seventh interaction, then all the credit was given to the final interaction and not previous ones. Now, with Facebook Analytics, you can see the entire path stretching from interaction to conversion instead of just the last point.

As soon as you open Facebook Analytics, you will be able to see an overview of all the data. Facebook Analytics has artificial intelligence capabilities, and it will display important data or insights like the users who engage most frequently with your content. It also provides omnichannel analytics, which helps you view all the users who switched from the Facebook app to your website or from your website to the Facebook app before conversion. It provides customized dashboards where you can view all the important data at once. It also enables you to create event source groups from the Analytics dashboard, thereby permitting you to segment and retarget all those users who followed a particular path of events on your page.

The information available is seemingly endless, but it will be useless if you do not know how to properly access and evaluate the data.

Step 1: Accessing Facebook Analytics

Go to the Facebook Analytics dashboard. You must install Facebook Pixel if you want to access this dashboard. Once you install the pixel and allow it to run, your Analytics dashboard will be full of analytical data.

When you open the dashboard, you can see the overview of all the data. Click on the "Dashboards" option, and you can see the custom dashboards as well as the omnichannel dashboard. If you want to learn more about the analytics related to a specific set of users, funnels, purchases, or anything else, then you must click on the "Activity" option. You can start adding any relevant charts to the custom dashboard; this will give you easier access when searching for data.

You can also pin any important data onto your dashboard. To do this, you must click on the icon "Pin to a Dashboard" that is present on the chart you want to pin. You can also pin a chart to a custom dashboard. To do this, you must either select an existing dashboard or opt for the "Create a New Dashboard" option. Once you do this, you must type the name of the chart you want to pin and click on the option "Add to the Dashboard."

Step 2: Reviewing activity reports

The activity reports form the basis of this analytics software. They help you understand all the collected data according to your needs to help make better decisions. The Analytics dashboard has comprehensive reporting features. You can delve as deep into the data as you want, and you can also view micro-conversions along with the global events and demographics.

For instance, if you are an owner of an e-commerce store, and you wish to determine the users who are converting from Facebook then you must go to Choose Activity Revenue, and it will provide a report of all the data related to purchases. To further filter the data, you must select an option from the "Show By" drop-down menu displayed. You can click on the "Traffic Source" option from the drop-down menu to view all the conversions according to the traffic source.

Another brilliant aspect about Facebook Analytics is you can design cross-channel funnels to decide on the interaction paths reporting the highest rate of conversion. If you wish to create a funnel, you must click on "Activity" then open "Funnels" and select the option "Create Funnel" present on the page. Here are a couple of examples of funnels you can use:

- Users who installed your app and then used your website to make a purchase.

- Users who used your website to make a purchase but messaged your Facebook page before making the purchase.

- Users who interacted with a specific Facebook post before making a purchase.

- Users who reacted in a specific manner while interacting with a post before making a purchase.

You can make the funnel as detailed or as simple as you want it to be.

Step 3: Using Facebook Analytics data

The real advantage of using Facebook Analytics is that it provides you with all the data you will need to make better and more informed decisions for your business. It is essential that you understand the data to improve your Facebook ad campaigns.

For instance, if one of your Facebook ad campaigns encourages users to click but not to convert then the users might start to interact with a retargeting campaign that is showing better conversions. Without the first campaign, you will not be able to reach the point that finally led to conversions.

So how can you use all this data to your advantage? You can identify the funnels that are showing a good rate of conversion and then concentrate your efforts to increase the flow of users through that funnel. For instance, if you observe that most of the users convert after messaging your Facebook page, you can start using Messenger chatbots to engage with those who like your page. Or if you notice that users are converting better after interacting with your posts, you can take steps to improve the chances of such interactions.

You can get as creative as you want while using the data from Facebook Analytics. If you are smart about it, the data you collect can help you identify your ideal target audience, the place and position of your ads, the channels to which you must divert the traffic, and also the kinds of content you must post. Spend some time and explore all the features of Facebook Analytics. Go through all the data reports carefully, target different sets of the audience, and use various combinations of funnels. Your understanding of Analytics will improve as you spend more time using it.

Metrics to Track

Facebook provides a lot of data, and it can be rather overwhelming if you cannot differentiate between the important and not-so-important data. Here are the best metrics you should track on Facebook.

Engagement

Engagement helps track the number of times a user acts on your Facebook posts. It can refer to actions like sharing a post, clicking on the associated link or event, leaving a comment, or any other type of interaction. Engagement is amongst the most useful metrics to track because it helps gauge whether the users like the content you post or not.

It might also increase the exposure of your posts. Facebook's algorithm is designed such that it determines the positioning of your posts on the follower's feed. The algorithm displays posts according to the interests of the users. If a specific post of yours receives a lot of engagement, it signals to the Facebook algorithm that your post is popular, and the likelihood of it popping up in your follower's news feed increases.

Relevance score

This is a Facebook metric that helps you measure the relevancy of your ads according to your target audience. This is usually measured on a scale of one to 10. A low score means your ads are barely relevant to your target audience, and a high score of 10 means the ads are quite relevant. This is a very important metric if you want to see how your Facebook campaigns are performing. If the relevancy score is low, then it means the frequency with which Facebook shows the ads will be quite low, and it directly increases your cost per click. On the other hand, a high score relating to relevance will increase how often it is shown and even reduce your overall costs. Reach and fan reach are the two alternatives of this metric.

Impressions

Impressions refer to the number of times your Facebook ads or posts have been seen. This applies to organic and paid-for Facebook content.

You cannot get any clicks if no one views your content. Impressions help diagnose the performance of your ads. If other metrics in the funnel, like clicks or conversions, aren't performing like you hoped they would, then you can use impressions to see how well the content is performing. The detailed metrics to this is Likes, Comments, and Engagement.

Leads generated

This refers to the number of potential customers you have gained via Facebook. This can come in several forms ranging from getting a user to sign up for a newsletter to having them provide their email in exchange for an eBook preview. Facebook helps you generate leads, and Facebook ads offer several built-in tools for generated leads within Facebook. All of this makes it easier for your targeted users to express their interest and for your content to generate leads.

ROAS

ROAS stands for return on an ad spend, and it denotes the return you stand to receive for every dollar you spend on advertising on Facebook. It measures the income you are generating through conversions via your Facebook ads.

Why does this metric matter? You might have shelled out a lot of money on your Facebook ads, but you still might not have gotten very far. ROAS helps ensure your media budget is helping you attain the results you want.

ROAS is calculated by dividing your total ad cost by the total number of website conversions you get. For instance, if you were spending $1,000 on your advertising campaign per month and managed to generate a revenue of $4,000 in that month, then your ROAS will be 4:1. This means that for every dollar you have spent, you stand to gain $4. If your

ROAS is positive, it means you are making money, and if it is negative, your ad campaign is not successful and is incurring a loss. This helps you allocate your marketing budget accordingly to focus on campaigns that are making you more money. This can also include other similar metrics like cost per conversion or cost per action.

Video metrics

The different video metrics you must track are the view through rate, video retention, and video engagement. Video view through rate refers to the number of users your video reached and how many of those users viewed the video. A video view means a user has viewed the video for at least three seconds. If you have an audience of 10,000 users and 3,000 of the users viewed the video, it means your video view rate is 30%. Anything less than 30% means your videos aren't doing as well as they are supposed to.

If you are publishing a 7-minute long video, but most of your audience only views about 30-seconds of it, then you must consider cutting down on the video length. As with the regular Facebook posts, you can also measure the video engagement you receive. By checking the number of likes, comments, shares, or any other engagement metric for videos, you can gauge whether the videos are effective or not.

Conversions

Conversion refers to the number of times your intended audience has taken an action you wanted them to. This can include an action like purchasing on your website, registering for your newsletter, or any other related activities. The goal of any marketing campaign is to increase conversions. By measuring conversions, you can optimize your campaign to reach your goal.

You have the option to select "conversions" as your whole goal. This creates a campaign on Facebook Ads where the program will automatically optimize your campaign to meet your goal. It ensures your budget is directed toward increasing conversions instead of focusing on other goals like clicks or impressions.

Ad frequency

This refers to the number of times your ad was viewed by a user. This is calculated by dividing the total impressions per ad (the number of times your ad was shown) by its total reach (the number of users who viewed your ad). If your reach stays dormant while the impressions increase, it means there is an increase in your ad frequency. The more a user views your ad without taking the necessary action, the less likely it is that they will convert, as a Facebook ad often interrupts the user's experience.

If a user is not interested in your ad even after viewing it a couple of times, it is unlikely that said user will develop an interest in what you are advertising. If you continue to keep showing the ads to uninterested users, you will merely be increasing your marketing costs.

Click-through rate

The click-through rate or CTR helps measure the percentage of users who clicked through to the landing page after viewing the ad. This is an important metric while measuring the performance of your marketing campaigns by directing clicks to a specific page or landing page. Clicks can help measure this, but they don't provide data on whether your targeted audience is interacting with your ads as desired or not. High CTR means users are taking the desired action, and it means you did well while selecting your target audience as well as choosing the ads you are showing them. A low CTR means the opposite of that.

Cost per click

Cost per click or CPC refers to the average cost incurred while earning one click on your Facebook campaign. You can calculate CPC by dividing your total ad budget by the total number of clicks you receive. However, to measure the effectiveness of CPC, you must take your ad budget into account.

For instance, you might be running two ad campaigns on Facebook. One campaign receives 1,000 clicks, and the other receives only 100. The one with 1,000 clicks must be doing better. Well, that's not necessarily true. If the cost of the first campaign is $1,000 and the other is only $50, then your answer about the CPC will change. The CPC of the first campaign is $1, while that of the second campaign is only $0.50.

Best performing ads

This shows the ads that are performing well and are earning the most impressions, clicks, or conversions. The success of a Facebook ads campaign depends on monitoring and optimizing that information by closely monitoring the ads, you can see for yourself which of the techniques is working well with your target audience. Once you have this information, you can start removing the ads that aren't doing too well and create content for future ads based on the content of the ads that are doing well.

Start Tracking Your Facebook Metrics

Apart from using Facebook Analytics to track metrics, you can use other third-party apps too. Below is a list of the best apps you can use for getting started.

Likealyzer

This is a free tool that is easy to use. You can open any Facebook page and then measure or analyze its effectiveness. This tool grades a page on the total score of 100 and then compares it with other similar pages. This means you can easily obtain a preview of your competitor's pages. It gives you the required metrics and some suggestions for changes. The metrics it provides include the rate of engagement, the length of posts, as well as the timing of the posts.

SimplyMeasured

SimplyMeasured offers four different Facebook reports. The four reports are an Insights Analysis report, a Competitive Analysis report, a Fan Page Analysis report (a fan page is the same as a business page), and a Content Analysis report. The Insights report prepares the data provided by Facebook Insights into various forms of charts. The information included within the reports relates to reach, stories, follower statistics and demographics, follower activity, page likes, impressions, and engagement. The program allows you to compare pages of similar companies or brands. It presents all the metrics in the form of charts.

The Fan Page report provides detailed information about content metrics, community, and project metrics. The top users are classified according to the number of posts, comments, and overall engagement. The Content Analysis report analyzes the breakdown of content you share including the types of messages, their engagement, and general keywords.

Soziograph.io

After receiving the necessary authorizations, you can use this tool to analyze every Facebook fan page for free. It displays the average number of likes, shares, and comments received from each post; the different types of posts; and the top posts for a specific period. You can return to the news since the page was created. It is certainly easy to use, but it doesn't provide a lot of actionable data like the other tools.

Quintly

This is a very powerful tool that allows you to create detailed analyses of different social networking platforms. It helps you track your business on social networks like Facebook, Twitter, YouTube, Google+, LinkedIn, and Instagram. Quintly also helps you compare the features that allow you to compare performance with the competitor and industry metrics. The Quintly toolbar also offers customization options so you can focus only on statistics that are the most important to you instead of worrying about all the other ancillary statistics.

Agorapulse

It offers two free Facebook tools. The first tool helps you set a benchmark for the kind of content you want to create. You can then compare this with other pages to see their performance. It helps you measure if your content is above average and helps track the associated metrics. The second tool lets you run contests, quizzes, and lotteries on your Facebook timeline. It does this while tracking your response time to messages. This tool covers the most influential users and users who most frequently mention your brand. It provides page-level analytics, timeline-level analytics, and other detailed reports. On Facebook, you can see a detailed breakdown of the organic, paid, and viral coverage of your brand. This will help you understand which content is best for you. It also provides a return on investment calculator that helps you determine your marketing and advertising budget on Facebook. You can customize the reports it provides and even download them as a

PowerPoint presentation of 20 slides.

Chapter Ten
Sales Funnel

There are various options available when it comes to Facebook advertising. For instance, you can increase your brand awareness, improve the engagement rate, direct traffic from your Facebook page to a landing website or webpage, and even increase the rate of conversions. The benefits you receive essentially depend on the specific goals you want to achieve. However, Facebook is quite different from Adwords or other conventional PPC platforms. Basically, Facebook is so much more than just buying impressions or clicks. If you use Facebook optimally, you can create an excellent sales funnel.

Before delving into all of it, you must answer a simple question: What is your purpose when you log into your Facebook profile? Are you merely there to check the updates of your friends and to check about the general news or do you log into Facebook to search for products and purchase them? Chances of it being the former are greater than the latter.

Facebook is more about socializing and networking than buying. Seldom does a Facebook user think about purchasing while going through their Facebook feed. This all means the overall intent of buying displayed by Facebook users is quite low. This may make you wonder, what is the point of using Facebook marketing and ads to grow your business if Facebook users are particularly interested in shopping.

Well, this might be the case for some brands that end up being rather disappointed with their ROI. They might acquire new followers, increase their engagement, and such but their rate of conversions doesn't improve. The important thing to remember is that this problem isn't with Facebook; it instead lies in the approach marketers adopt while using Facebook. Hard selling on Facebook is not a good idea. You must create a good sales funnel if you want to generate positive results from your Facebook marketing and advertising campaign.

Creating a Sales Funnel

Before learning about creating an optimal sales funnel on Facebook, you must learn about the different stages a potential buyer goes through before making a purchase. A buying cycle includes the recognition of an opportunity, discovery of alternatives, comparison of solutions, making a decision, and implementing the solution. If a potential buyer is in the stage of opportunity recognition, it is unlikely that such a person will immediately skip to the purchase stage. However, there will be some customers who will be ready to purchase. That said, a majority of Facebook users don't intend to make a purchase when they log into their Facebook accounts. This is where you must try to gently coax them to make a purchase. The best way to go about this is by developing a sales funnel. Here are the steps you must follow to create a good sales funnel.

Step one: Creating segmented content

To start with, you must have a couple of different types of content available. It can be in the form of videos, infographics, blog posts, webinars, eBooks, or even slideshows. The specific path you opt for doesn't matter much as long as you provide content which is engaging, relevant, and high-quality. You must ensure that whatever you are promoting can be purchased on your website. This comes in handy when you start to retarget your leads to work them further along the sales funnel. You need different forms of content to reach different segments of your target audience.

You cannot depend on a one-size-fits-all approach because different individuals will be at different stages of the buying cycle. Some might

276

not be interested in making an immediate purchase and might be browsing through their options while others might be considering the idea of buying something. Once you have the right content according to the audience you are targeting, they will enter your sales funnel.

Step two: Promoting content to "warm audience"

You must start promoting your content to "warm audience." It essentially means you must target those users who have been exposed to your content or your brand in some way and have shown some level of interest in the same. This category of users will essentially comprise of your existing Facebook followers and can also include the list of users who have associated with your business or brand in the past. You must pay attention to the level of engagement and determine the type of content which leads to most purchases. Take some time, analyze the different metrics available to you, and make a note of the content that's doing well.

Step three: Targeting lookalike audiences

A lookalike audience is a term that's used to describe those users who share similar interests, behaviors, and habits like your existing target audience. You can think of them as a cold audience who can be easily warmed up to your brand and can be converted into potential leads. Therefore, you must ensure your marketing strategies target this section of the audience along with your core audience. If you want to do this, you must open Facebook ads, go to the Audience section of it, and click on the option "Create a Lookalike Audience." Once you do this, a pop-up will show up on your screen, and you need first to select the source. You can create a custom audience or use the data from a tracking pixel or page. Choose the source that is ideal for you.

The next step is to select the audience's location and size, which ranges from anywhere between 1% to 10% of the population in the area, country, or countries you choose. While selecting the audience size, keep in mind that the smaller the percentage, the more similar your lookalike audience will be to your existing audience. Once you select the necessary parameters, the next step is to click on "Create Audience" option. The lookalike audience thus created will be a part of the overall cold audience who need some persuasion to warm up to your brand or business.

Step four: Promoting the best content

Remember the content that your "warm audience" responded the most to in the previous steps? Now, you must use the same content and direct it toward your cold audience. The content can be in the form of a textual post, webinar, video, or anything else. If you do this carefully, then you will be able to appeal to your cold audience and can introduce them to your sales funnel, and they will become a part of your warm audience. After doing all this, the cold audience will now become aware of your brand and will have some inclination about making a purchase.

Step five: Remarketing

While advertising on Facebook, it isn't realistic to expect a lot of people to switch from being your cold audience to being viable leads who are eager to make a purchase. Usually, your cold audience must be exposed to your brand multiple times before they are primed to purchase. So, how can you prime them and get them to move further along the sales funnel? The key to it is remarketing, and Facebook is the best platform for remarketing.

Step six: Using Facebook Pixel

You need to create a Facebook Pixel, add the pixel to your website's code, and use it to start remarketing and directing visitors back to your website to make a purchase. By using Facebook Pixel, you can start collecting all the important data you need to optimize any existing ads and to develop more effective ads in the future.

Step seven: Using videos

There are various ways in which you can start remarketing. However, while using Facebook, the best idea is to use videos to get your target audience to move along the sales funnel. Since you are dealing with "warm audience" at this point, it is quite likely that they might have been exposed to your content in one form or the other and are even a little interested in it. By using videos, you can help make a connection and encourage them to visit your desired landing page.

Marketing is all about encouraging your audience to delve a little deeper and get better acquainted with your brand. This is a subtle way of converting your target audience into viable leads without coming across as being pushy. For instance, if you have watched any of the videos made by fashion influencers on Facebook, you will notice that in most of their videos they not only acknowledge the viewer for watching the video but also tell their viewers to visit their landing page to learn more about the items mentioned in the video.

Step eight: Keep remarketing

You might be quite eager to make some conversions, but don't expect all your audience to convert. So, what can you do now? Now you need to come up with other ideas to remarket to your audience. Your intention at this point must be to reach out to those who haven't converted and encourage them to convert by offering them something of value in return. You can offer an informational product that you know will not only be liked by your audience but that they will find useful too.

279

You need to think of different ways in which you can get your audience to convert. Maybe you can offer them a free trial, an eBook, or anything else once they sign up. Offer them an incentive, and you are bound to increase their interest in your brand.

Step nine: Warming up your leads

It is great that you have managed to motivate a portion of your target audience to opt in. If you are using email lists to convert your audience into viable leads, remember that most people don't open or go through their emails. Maybe you were offering them a free eBook or a free trial, and someone didn't convert even after going through the informational product you offered them.

Now is the time to start warming up your leads once again. You can create an ad to explain the benefits of the product you are offering to gently nudge them to make a purchase. You can also include testimonials or anything else that you think will help increase the credibility of your brand. These things help the audience trust your brand and give them the motivation to make the purchase.

Step ten: Time to hard sell

The final step of the Facebook sales funnel is the hard sell. Yes, it is time to move on from all the subtle sales tactics used in the previous steps and go for the jugular. You will need to direct your attention to all those who used your free trial, downloaded the free eBook and so on but never made a purchase. The best way to goad this segment of users to make a purchase is by creating a personalized video ad that includes something along the lines of, "Thank you for checking out (the free content you offer), but for some reason, you did not complete your purchase (mention the product's name." Once you do this, it is time to go for the hard sell, and you can do this with the help of a not-so-subtle sales message about why they must make the purchase. By now, all your leads will be quite familiar with your brand and are as warmed up to your brand as they will ever be. It means they are primed, and they are ready to purchase!

Chapter Eleven
More About Facebook Ads

Carousel Advertisement

Before you can run ads on Facebook's carousel, you need a plan and strategy for your advertising campaign. Once you've decided on the message, image, and strategy you want to use, creating an ad is easy. You need to think about your target audience, what action it should take, and what gets your audience to take that action. You'll need to make a list of your customers and their interests, track down links to your website, and include high-quality videos or pictures that match your message.

Before you begin, review the recommended image size and other information listed on the Facebook Advertising Page. You can be inspired by the different formats of the advertising carousel. Then you can create the same layout in Creative Hub.

To create a carousel ad for your page, follow these steps:

- Click on the "Promote" button on the page and select "Get More Website Visitors."

- In the "Ad Creative" section present on the upper right side of the page, click on "Edit."

- Enter the desired URL that you want people to be directed to when they click on the ad. If you want each carousel card to send the visitor to a different URL, then you can edit the ad in Ads Manager.

- Once you do this, add the text for your ad.

- Click the + sign, under the Images section to add carousel cards.

- Click on the number of the card you want a particular image to be added to.

- Then click on "Upload Image" to add an image from your computer, or you can click on "Select Image" to upload an image from your library that you previously used.

- Click on "Reposition Image" if you want to crop the image.

- You need to add a headline for every card in the carousel.

- Click on the "Ad Creative" section and click on "Save" when you want to save the changes to the carousel.

- You'll then need to enter the required audience, budget and duration information, and the "Payment" section to fill out the ad. Then click on "Apply."

- Use an editor to create carousel advertisements.

One of the key benefits of using the Power Editor to create a carousel ad is that you can add more text to the ad. In Advertising Manager, you can use 25 characters for the title and approximately 90 characters for any text. If you use the Power Editor, you can add more text.

After starting your campaign and naming the ad set and ad, you can customize it in Power Editor. You will notice that the text contains no restrictions.

With the Power Editor, you can tell the audience the complete story about the topic.

You can also customize the display area of the URL. In this additional section, you can add additional text to the product or provide information about transactions. This feature comes in handy if the URL is long and cumbersome. For example, you can use additional tracking in the website URL and enter the actual website address in the Display URL field so that users know where they want to go.

If you would like to increase the call to action, you can mark the "Register" option in the URL display area.

In the Power Editor, you can mark other pages in the ad text. This helps make the ad look like a normal message, and it also increases visibility. If you mark other pages, make sure the tags are relevant. To mark another page or people in your ad, you must enter @ and then the name of the page or person in the text box and select the appropriate name from the drop-down menu. If you use organic content for advertising, tagging increases visibility.

There are two types of ads in the Power Editor: Product Displays and Carousels.

Up to five products can be displayed in the carousel displays configured in the Power Editor. Not only can you select the images that you want to appear on your ad, but you can also add a link to a unique website for each product. Each announcement in the carousel has its own description and a title.

For advertising carousels, the image size should be 600 x 600 pixels. Once you've made all the necessary changes to your ad, your ad will run.

Split Test

With split testing, you can evaluate the effectiveness of advertising and determine which ad, image, or format leads to the best results. Split tests provide statistical results.

If you want to split an ad on Facebook, you'll need to select the "Campaign Breakup" option when you select a destination for an ad campaign. The only two goals that are not yet available are brand awareness and shopping. The split function test lets you test the audience, place, and optimization rates.

Click "Create" on the Display toolbar. You can use Guided Creation instead of the Quick Creation stream the first time you use split tests.

Let's take an example to understand how split tests work. Imagine you have two ad formats, and you do not know which one to choose. This where you can use split tests. The target you want to test is the amount of traffic intended for everyone who viewed the content and should be directed to the appropriate web site. You must check the destination using the list specified in the split test box.

After selecting a goal, go to the ad group level and click "Creative" in the Variable section. You can create two promotional options: A and B. You can add up to 5 different ads at once if you select the "Check Other Ad" option.

Select your audience, placement, bid optimization, trial schedule, and budget from the rest of the ad set.

In the previous example, the idea was addressed to anyone watching video content. In the "Audience" section, you must select "Video" for the user groups. You can also select the page view or a website. If no user group is available for you, select Saved user groups, and Duplicate user groups.

You can choose from options for the placement, delivery, and optimization settings. You can select the default automatic placement option and optimize it for link clicks (another alternative is optimization for landing page views).

After that, you have to choose a budget and a schedule for the tests. You can do the test between 3 and 14 days. When the Ad Unit section has finished, click Next to go to the ad level.

Now you need to create all the variations of ads you want to test. For example, if you want to test the effectiveness of a carousel ad and an image ad, you must label ad A as a carousel ad. Then you have to select the Facebook page in the "Identify" section.

Next, you have to select the format of the carousel and fill in the ad. This means you need to promote pictures, headlines, links, and descriptions.

After you create Ad A, you can switch to Ad B. Click on "Switch to Display B." Facebook automatically fills in the data according to screen A. You will need to change some details to perform the test task. In this case, you have to change the format of the advertisement.

Since display A is a carousel display, display B is a single image display. So, choose the "Single Image" option in the "Ad Format" section, and then add the image you used in your first carousel. Add text, link, and CTA (if available), and make sure that any details you add here should match the map from the carousel advertisement you've created.

Then click on "Confirm," and you can see the campaign. Now you can successfully split your advertising test.

The "Creative Split Test" option allows you to match two ad formats. You can also use it to test ad copy options, headlines, action prompts, images, image-based carousel ads, video-based carousel ads, and video ads that are not related to other commercials.

The split-test option allows you to test various creative options to maximize the use of FB advertising.

Chapter Twelve
Tips to Create High-Quality Content

General Tips

When it comes to marketing on social media sites, content is king. You need to churn out high-quality content that your target audience will find appealing, entertaining, or empowering.

Consider everything

There is only one way to determine if your efforts are working effectively, and that is completing an evaluation of all data. Some social networking platforms have built-in tools to help you do that. There are many options available for third-party analysis tools. Use them to see what gets the most feedback on the content you've shared or promoted, and, equally importantly, what does not get the required level of response. That way, you can find out where you are successful and where you need to improve.

Make sure you publish at the right time

It is important to post content that engages your audience by prompting them to like, comment, or share. When it comes to optimizing this, the timing of your posts is very important because that determines how many people will see the post. Most business to business companies tend to post during normal business hours, but even then, posting on certain days will produce a much better response than posting on others. Do your homework to find out when your target audience is likely to be online and plan to post messages while they're there.

Create your connections

One of the common mistakes that social networking marketers make is talking at the audience, not with them. Talk to your followers and interact with them by responding to comments and messages or liking their content. They want to know that you are human and not just some kind of computer that provides automatic answers. Ask them to share their thoughts and make sure you respond in good time to their comments. If they send you messages, contact them immediately. If you effectively ignore potential customers, they will be driven out.

Go visual

People are repelled by large blocks of text, but they pause and pay attention to the pictures. Photos, videos, and infographics contain information that is easier to recognize for people. Make sure your visual content is strong, engaging, and relevant to your business.

Make each of your selected platforms unique

Many tools allow you to share content across multiple platforms, and this can be helpful for important information. However, if you do this for each piece of content, all of your platforms will be the same. People following you on a platform are likely to follow you on all platforms, and they do not want to see identical content. This ensures that they only follow you on one platform. Make each of your accounts unique, and you will attract more people and gain even more followers and more potential customers.

Let people follow you

If someone subscribes to you on the social network, he wants to thank you. Offer bonuses for a subscription or a like such as a small discount on a product or a raffle. People need an incentive to join you, and providing perks for following you will keep them interested in continuing to follow you.

Remember to be personable but professional

While social networking can be a more relaxed way of marketing your business, you still need to maintain an atmosphere of professionalism. Yes, give out some personal information that will give your business a human face, such as birthday announcements of employee fun facts, but never express your personal views on things on your business page. When you start thinking about politics or talking about the latest celebrity tricks, you can easily start turning your followers away from you.

Social media manager

Not everyone can handle social networks well, and if you can't, it's better to have someone at the helm who can easily communicate, interact, publish, and share with others. In this way, you will be able to continue your business and take advantage of a successful marketing campaign.

If it does not work, let go

Not everything will work; no matter how much analysis you carry out or how many new team members you hire, there is bound to be a platform that is not right for your business. If nothing works and you get no results, drop it and go. There are better things to focus your time and energy on.

Build business relationships

If there are companies that belong to the same industry or the same niche as you, join them and follow them, but only if they are not direct competitors. You can connect clients, share subscribers, and get tips. You may wonder how much benefit you can derive from it. Interacting with other companies can attract their followers to your brand or business. It's a great way to network and increase your reach.

Fight trolls

The more successful you become, the more attention your social media accounts attract. With that fame inevitably come internet trolls. Trolls often get into fights with other followers and post hateful and upsetting comments. If you find your page contains trolls or people who only want to cause trouble, handle them professionally. Do not engage in a negative manner with them because this will reflect poorly on you. At the same time, don't allow them to post whatever they want because they may run off other followers.

Don't keep selling

Facebook is perceived as a domain where people engage in a kind of social activity, chat with their friends, view photos and videos of others, and relax. They want to engage in conversation and become part of the community, not be bombarded by "outsiders" who are trying to aggressively sell products.

There are certain hard sales tactics that you should avoid. These include the use of advertising slogans, sending multiple messages about a specific

292

product or service, and providing redundant information about a product or service unrelated to a conversation. Your subscribers can unfollow you, but they can also do even worse: leave bad feedback about your business on your page. As a public page, these poor reviews can be seen by anyone who visits your page. Poor reviews will only hurt you.

Always have a clear goal

It is very important to have a clear goal in mind while using Facebook and a clearly defined strategy to achieve that goal. For example, a café can easily decide that its goal is to increase sales generated through Facebook by 10% within six months. The strategy could then include creating daily posts that use a coupon code to display unique specials or deals of the day so you can track a specific sale on Facebook. You can post a photo of the buyer with a cup of coffee at your café. You can also encourage users to post their photos (for example, in a coffee shop or with a small amount of coffee) to attract more attendees. Setting a goal as well as a strategy helps you to determine the direction and achieve the desired success.

Human side

In general, a Facebook user wants to communicate with another person and not engage in conversation with an impersonal company. Regardless of who is responsible for managing the Facebook page of a business or brand, that person should be able to write and develop content that communicates the "human" side of the business. Facebook gives you the chance to be more informal and lighthearted when interacting with customers. Do not make things sound too formal or hard.

Be regular

Unlike other media such as television, magazines, newspapers, etc., social networks allow you to include regular updates. Most Facebook users generally review their pages at least once a day, so you need to make sure your company publishes new content. Depending on your audiences' demographics, you can decide how often and when to post new content. Be regular, but don't go overboard.

Encouraging comments

You should encourage Facebook users to respond to your posts or comment on your posts about your business or its topic. When a user posts something, make sure that their message is answered within 24 hours. Refusing an answer can be seen as a lack of interest on your part. If you do not respond, you may not be tracked by users.

Use pictures and videos

One of the most attractive elements of Facebook is the fact that users can post photos and videos. Take advantage of this ability to keep your followers interested and engaged. As discussed in previous chapters, there are multiple ways to do this. For example, a chain of clothing stores may post images of a new inventory as it arrives, or a personal trainer may post a training video with instructions on how to perform a particular exercise.

Try to be as interactive as possible and attract your audience by holding various contests, conducting polls, creating quotes, and so on. Facebook should be fun, so you should include the fun element in your marketing strategies.

The two most common reasons why a user visits a business page on

Facebook are discounts and gifts. Competitions and games can make your site exciting. Customer surveys can be conducted via Facebook. If you want to do a survey, make the questions easy and make the survey short. Facebook facilitates short bursts of engagement, so try not to post long updates or surveys.

Develop relationships

It takes some time to build good relationships with other Facebook users, so you have to be patient. Try to get to know your followers. Take time to interact with them in the comments. You can like their comments or respond to them directly. Building relationships with your followers will make them more likely to continue a relationship with you.

Remember to use Facebook Insights

With Facebook Insights, you can better understand those who love your site and want to follow you. Once you know the characteristics of those who follow you, you can tailor your messages to their needs and their interests. For example, if a bookstore serves customers of all ages, but most subscribers are between 18 and 25 years old, the offers shared on Facebook should be designed according to that target audience of 18- to 25-year-olds. The offers in the store, however, should be more diverse.

Interaction

Make sure that you post actively on Facebook and engage in other ways. The more users come into contact with you, the more they will remember you. This can be achieved by posting content throughout the week. Use analytics to figure out when and how often to post, and don't be afraid to try different strategies. It can take time to figure out what best serves your audience. Once you find the sweet spot, you should see your engagement and follower count increase.

Tags are important

Tags allow you to identify who is in a certain post or picture. For example, in a picture of your employees, tagging each person will make it possible for followers to identify them and visit the employees' personal pages. Tagging someone in something will also make that content show up on their personal timeline. This increases the number of people who see your content. Don't overdo it though. Too many tags can be overwhelming.

Do not forget the commentators

This point cannot be stressed enough. Always remember to answer direct comments, opinions, and questions. Let your followers know that their opinions are important and that someone is paying attention to them. You may think it is best to ignore a critical comment or complaint, but remember that others can see your failure to respond. That doesn't reflect well on you.

Make sure your company profile is complete

You have enough room in your profile to give your subscribers a lot of information about you. It may seem tedious to fill in so many sections, but all of those sections contain information your followers want to know. The more detailed your profile, the better your audience will understand who you are and what you do. Remember that your Facebook page appears in Google search results and may be the first thing people come across when looking for your company. Don't leave them with unanswered questions after they visit your page. Make it as complete as possible.

Make sure your subscribers want to see your updates

The ultimate goal of a marketing plan is to get people to read your content. You want these people to cling to every word you write and strive to see what you will post next. You want them to check to see if you have published something recently. You can do this only with high quality, valuable, and relevant content.

Make it easier to share your content.

While the age of technology has allowed us to do as little as possible while still being productive, you need to work if you want your content to be engaging. You need to pack your content in a way that makes it easy to share and then give people the buttons they need to send content to a friend or other user on their social networking sites. Make it so easy for them that it's almost harder for them not to do it.

If you share something, comment on it

Do not just click the button that lets you share a post and leave it at that. Add a comment to let others know why you think content is worth sharing. This helps you build your own experience and reputation as an expert. This, in and of itself, increases the value of what you share.

Check your grammar and spelling

Texting lingo may be popular, but grammar and spelling are still important. You are a professional business, and the worst thing you can do is to publish content that is poorly written and contains mistakes. Review your work, then review it again. Make sure it meets professional standards before hitting send.

Learn the rules of the platform

Look at the recommendations for each platform and make sure you know what is acceptable and not acceptable in terms of behavior and content. Common sense should determine the nature of the content. You must review the platform's terms of service before publishing. Some platforms, especially Facebook, are constantly changing their rules for conducting competitions, and their violation may result in removed content, suspensions, or total exclusion from the platform. This is not what you want for your business.

Strategies for Facebook Pages

When it comes to promoting and using your page on Facebook, it's best to use page-only strategies to increase your appeal. This means that you will be posting exclusive offers on your Facebook page rather than publishing them elsewhere.

Below are some Facebook strategies that you can use.

Product

It's a good idea to start with the goods. This includes offering exclusive products that are not available in the store. For example, you can offer a full product that can only be purchased through your Facebook page or website, but not in a store. You can also offer an individual product that is exclusively available online. For example, you may suggest customizing the product by changing the color scheme or encrypting a message. You can also suggest a product in a color scheme or pattern that differs from the one available in the store. You must make this clear by making relevant announcements and telling your customers that they are exclusively online. You can also ask people in your store to like it online to get your "page" noticed.

Deals

You can make exclusive online deals. You can offer programs like "buy 1, get 1 for free" or include a bonus gift or a surprise coupon. Such offers will certainly attract interest and increase the value of your site. Again, it is important to promote this so that people know about the offer. You can send emails with details and inform others about the offers you have made to your online audience. You can also promote it in your store or distribute flyers to people telling them to visit your Facebook page for special information.

Awards

You can reward people who bring likes. This works well because people are being asked to get more and more people to like your site. The reward should be attractive enough to arouse the interest of your audience. You can offer coupons, free goods, or specially designed goods. Make these deals specific to Facebook users. You can place an ad on both the page and your other social networks telling them to visit your page to be eligible. You can also mention this on your website and inform people who visit your store.

Discount coupons

You can offer your customers discount vouchers and special coupons or codes. These vouchers give you a discount on the goods and services you offer in your store. You can only use these coupons on the Facebook page. Again, you must announce this on all your social networks, such as Twitter and Instagram, to let people know about what is happening.

Competitions

Competitions are a fun way to get people to visit your site and encourage them to interact with you. You can announce the contest on your Facebook page. The competition may be associated with products or services you offer. It could be something like asking your followers to create a slogan, come up with a phrase, or post product photos. Make sure the prize is desirable enough to entice people to actually participate in the competition. Set a short time limit for the competition, such as a week, to encourage immediate engagement and quickly increase followers.

Events

You can also announce upcoming company events on the pages. These can be events where people meet and get to know each other better. Such events also help you get to know your audience better because you can interact with them in person. Providing free refreshments or some other free gift is a great way to encourage attendance.

Events can help you a lot if done correctly. All you have to do is create an interesting event, invite as many people as you can, and spread the information on your page. Try to use the event to promote your company and your product. This has the advantage where you do not have to spend a lot of money on sponsorship events organized by other people. Many people sponsor local events to gain recognition for names. You can use Facebook to get name recognition without spending a lot of money on events. Events can spread beyond just your target audience if you make them public and invite many people. First, determine the type of event and when your target audience is most likely to be able. Start inviting people immediately to help spread the word as fast as possible. Give ample notice before the event. Announcing it with too short notice is a great way to host an event that no one attends.

Chapter Thirteen
Build a Community

Importance of Building Community

Facebook is not about people; it's about the community. Facebook is a means of communicating with other people, and that's the goal of the platform. It is a global social platform to meet like-minded people. The Facebook community helps to raise the visibility of your business or brand, promote your product or service, and drive your business. So, it's important to create a community for your business on Facebook.

It is not all about you

Most businesses will eventually face the pressure of having to maximize their sales via some sort of marketing strategy, and Facebook is one way to do this. But you must understand that Facebook communities are not a place for you to keep delivering your sales pitch.

Groups on Facebook are not created to solely serve your interests. Your community might or might not be a part of your target audience. You can determine whether a group is your target audience or a part of your Facebook community by this simple test: Check how the conversations flow. If the conversations essentially flow between you and the other members of the group, then they are your audience. If the conversations primarily take place between the members, then they are just a part of your Facebook community.

The Facebook community is made up of people who build relationships based on their shared goals, experiences, or interests. Your community is only part of your market, and those who are a part of it will obviously be interested in all that you offer. You must opt for such users who have had some past experience with your brand or business and whose USP matches yours. Please remember that the focus of the community must be on creating shared relationships and not on your business. You can act as a facilitator, but you must not try to hijack any conversations. Your role is the role of the facilitator, and your goal is for the conversations to grow. You can do this by asking questions and encouraging conversations. You need to get to know everyone in your community better. You can do this by welcoming people, sharing your common needs, showing patience, and waiting for that connection to continue.

Exclusivity

Who does not like the feeling of exclusivity? Everyone likes it when they feel they have exclusive access to something. A Facebook page is the official profile for an entity like a celebrity, a business, a brand, or even an organization, while a Facebook Group is a place for communication consisting of other users who share common interests and opinions. Groups allow users to come together according to a common cause they believe in, to express their opinions, or to even share related content.

Well, that's a great thing in Facebook groups. Exclusiveness helps build closer relationships not only with other members on Facebook but with other businesses too. For instance, don't you feel quite "cool" if you have a membership to an exclusive club? Well, the same logic applies to Facebook communities. The more exclusive the group is, the more the members will have in common, and their participation will naturally increase. You can control access by entering specific registration rules and checking participants before you accept them. The result of all this? The participants feel part of something exclusive.

You may wonder why this is important. Well, participants are encouraged to discuss and promote your business, and you do not even have to offer them information. They automatically assume the role of spokespersons for your brand or business.

Avoid being a salesperson

When it comes to making purchases, people are picky. Most customers prefer the recommendations given by their peers as opposed to professionally authored content. User-generated content is certainly more effective than the ones that the brand creates. By nature, people tend to trust their peers more than a business or a brand. Community members automatically support your brand or business if they feel that they are welcome and their support is acknowledged.

Do not air dirty laundry

Please remember your role as a community manager is to moderate and stimulate discussion. Participants should feel that the community is a place where they can share their views without judgment. The members need to be able to share their views and opinions on the topics related to the community page. If there are discrepancies in a community, as a community manager you must have a plan to dispel a heated discussion quickly. You must closely monitor the activities of the group and have someone who reacts quickly and sensitively to differences. Do not use the group as a means of sharing your own strong opinions, though. Remain and neutral and professional presence.

Welcome others

You need to introduce new members to the community. When you accept new members, you need to show them some love. You need new members who feel welcome, and you should be prepared to engage them in discussions. You can do this by selecting some standard questions that you can ask them as soon as they become part of the group. This helps in making the new members feel welcome.

Loyalty

Members of a strong community want four things:

- A feeling of exclusivity

- To benefit from the community

- To create an emotional bond

- To fulfill their needs

The participants of a Facebook community must be able to recognize each other easily, and to do this you can create logos or something similar. Participants should feel that their opinions are being heard and acknowledged. To make someone feel like their suggestions are being acknowledged, you can thank them for their support or even implement some of their suggestions. Recognition and reward are the best way to encourage participation. Building a loyal community for your brand will automatically translate into a better conversion. To keep up with all this, it would be nice to have group policies and understand the usual group jargon.

If you want to increase positive activity in the group, you need to include public praise. If you praise someone, be sure to thank him. You can send them a postcard, chocolate, or anything else that conveys the message, "Thank you for being a valuable member of the community."

Community

Your community helps with indirect sales, and you need to optimize it. The four elements you need to focus on are social listening, social influence, social networking, and social selling.

Social listening is monitoring, responding, and caring for customers on a social platform. Social influence is the creation of authority on social media platforms through the dissemination of useful and practical content. Social networking refers to the search for influential people to promote your brand. Social selling is an indirect search for potential customers that leads to conversion.

To increase sales, build brand awareness, build a strong audience, and increase conversion rates, you need a strong community.

Chapter Fourteen
Facebook Stories and Facebook Live

Facebook Stories

If you want to share your adventures with all your friends and followers on Facebook, you need to use Facebook Stories. This is better than downloading a picture because it offers several options for playing the photos or videos you want to share. It's important that your advertising campaign keeps pace with the latest updates and features on Facebook.

The stories on Facebook are very similar to the news feed, but one difference between the two is that the first one is more visual. The user can add various filters and effects to the camera and publish them in the Stories section instead of downloading them as normal messages. Stories you create on Facebook can be shared with a group of people or even a single user. Once the story is published, it will be available within 24 hours and then disappear. This is very similar to Snapchat Stories.

To prepare your photos for Facebook stories, you have three options. Open the Facebook app on your mobile phone, tap the "Your Story" icon, and then tap the "Camera" icon at the top left of the screen. Then you need to press the record button to take a photo or video. If you want to share an existing photo, you can download it from the camera.

If you want to use this feature on your desktop, you will need to create a message for each publication in the news feed as usual. Once it's done, you'll need to add it to your story instead of downloading it as a regular post.

Facebook introduced the Facebook Story feature in 2017. If you want your brand or business to feel fashionable and cool, you need to be aware of any new developments that they represent.

Facebook Business Practice History

Facebook Story is a clone of Snapchat Stories or Instagram Stories. You must ensure that you are familiar with this practice before using it on your corporate site. The first thing you need to do is check before using, examine all the buttons and their functions, and then do a quick test drive.

As a business owner, you are a representative of your business, and your Facebook ad should reflect the same. This applies to not only your news but also your stories. You must make sure that the emojis, filters, colors, borders, text colors, and hashtags you use are brand oriented. Try to demonstrate your brand voice in a fun and creative way.

You must regularly and frequently publish stories on Facebook. With Facebook stories, you can quickly take a look at everything that happens to you and your business. If you want to provide your subscribers and friends with exciting updates, choose Facebook Stories. You should consider the time at which most of your subscribers will be online and then publish it accordingly. You can also extend the story at any time. You need to make sure that the content you upload reaches your audience. If this is not the case, this completely contradicts the purpose of advertising.

Keep in mind that all subscribers on your corporate page will see the history. Stories are an easy way for most people to make a personal connection with the audience. So, remember, it's all about making a personal connection without overloading you with business issues. You need to find the perfect balance between business and personal communication. Share a few posts that are fun or easy and include them in some business-related posts.

Your Facebook followers are always on the lookout for something genuine and interesting. You are a representative of your company, but do not forget to give your audience something that captivates them. You can develop and improve your relationships with online users with Facebook Stories. To make the stories look a bit more individual, you can add selfies, post pictures of interesting events of the day, provide a quick overview of what's going on, or even add some quotes or "deep thoughts." For example, if you have a big ad or big event planned for the future, you can use Facebook Stories for daily updates.

One thing you should never forget when using advertising on Facebook is that people go to Facebook because it is fun and interesting to them. So, you need to make sure your Facebook stories meet these simple criteria. The best way to make people happy with your updates is to give them something valuable. The content needs to entertain users, offer them ideas they cannot get from anyone, share things that make them feel valuable, and show them the private side of your business that's just for Facebook Stories.

Now that you are informed about Facebook Stories, the next step is to integrate it into your advertising campaign successfully.

Facebook Live

Nowadays, live video has become a popular form of advertising, and Facebook has responded to that with a new tool, Facebook Live.

Facebook Live is a streaming video option from Facebook. You can stream a live video to your audience about your business profile or personal profile. Launched in April 2016, Facebook Live is very popular with online marketers and advertisers today.

Once you create a video from Facebook Live, it stays on your page or profile, so anyone who missed the live broadcast can still see it. The video will be displayed during and after the event in the user's news feed. You may be wondering why a company should use this feature. Here are a few of the reasons that will prompt you to include Facebook live video in your ad campaign:

- This helps a company to connect with its audience sincerely and gives the brand a personal feel. If you have ever felt that the audience tends to view your brand as a corporate robot, you can change that with this feature.

- You can easily interact with your users in real time and answer their questions. It allows you to interact with your viewers if they are interested.

- You can use Facebook Live to demonstrate the event to anyone who cannot attend the event. It helps you to connect with your customers and subscribers.

- You can also share industry updates.

- Facebook Live also helps you to demonstrate your corporate culture. This is the perfect way to give your brand a sense of humanity.

When should Facebook Live be used?

You need to know when you can use Facebook Live. There are certain cases where a video on Facebook Live works better than a normal post. This section offers suggestions about what to consider when using Facebook Live and when it is most appropriate.

If you want to introduce the audience to the experience of your business or brand, use Facebook Live. This only works if you have a physical storefront. It conveys the appearance of your business or employees that you cannot convey with texts or images.

Use this feature when you want to conduct events or webinars. A well-planned webinar is an easy way to reach potential customers.

This is the perfect tool for hosting a question and answer session that you want your audience to be engaged in. If you can interact with your viewers in real time, then that has more impact than normal text conversations on the Internet. When planning and reporting on a Q & A session, you can attract many of your viewers. This helps to build a better relationship.

Use Facebook Live to offer online classes. Information is the most valuable asset today. If you can provide free and valuable information, you can create a loyal audience. The public will want to visit your site more often if you can offer them something valuable.

Product release is pretty intriguing. If you are planning a product launch, do not forget to transfer it to Facebook Live. It is also a good customer service platform.

To start a Facebook live event

Now that you know what Facebook Live is, the next step is to use it. This section tells you the simple steps you need to take to get started. You will need a mobile phone or desktop with a good camera and a microphone to start a Facebook live event.

The first step is to click the "Live Video" button. If you use Facebook on your mobile phone, a small button will appear when composing a post that says "Live Video." Click here to start. If you're using the desktop, Live Video appears in the Publish window.

The next step is to write an attractive description. The description, along with the thumbnail video, is the most important parts of the video. Without convincing content, you cannot entice viewers into watching videos. When writing a copy, make sure it is direct, effective, and informative. Try to give the viewer the information he needs but hold some content back to create a sense of curiosity.

Once you've done all this, it's time to take a stand and act. If you want to record some type of series, try to be consistent with your location. You must use the same set if it is a repeating series. So, choose a place carefully.

Use an external microphone to improve sound quality.

When finished, click Finish and the stream will stop. Make sure you completed the session correctly and did not forget to stop the stream.

After the live broadcast ends, your video will continue to be broadcast to all viewers who missed the live broadcast. You can share the video on the page and even make the necessary changes to it.

Using Facebook Live with a desktop computer

If you want to use Facebook Live on your desktop, you'll need to open the browser of your choice and then visit Facebook.com.

Touch the status text box on the screen, then tap Live video.

Enter a brief description for the live video, select your privacy settings, and click "Next." When prompted, click "Allow" to grant Facebook the necessary permissions to access the webcam and microphone. After doing this, you need to click on "Go Live," and the live feed will start.

Before, during, and after Facebook Live

There are some things you need to do before, during, and after posting on Facebook Live.

First, you need to promote the event before streaming live video. It's important to understand that a live video is very similar to an event and not a blog post. You can always follow the content you posted with consistent advertising, but for live video, the action takes place before the actual event. In other words, you need to generate enough news for viewers to see the video. With Facebook, you can use your promotions to target specific events and groups. You'll need to post your upcoming ad on your Facebook page as often as possible. This means that you need to share daily broadcast updates. You need to communicate something valuable if you remind the audience of this event. Promote the live event on other social networks of your company to attract a large audience.

You must limit any distractions if you opt for Facebook Live. Yes, Facebook Live is certainly more relaxed and offers a natural experience compared to traditional advertising. However, this does not mean that you should not plan ahead of time. You need to remember that you represent the brand, and what you do in live broadcasting affects your brand and your business. That's why it's important that you always put your company's best foot forward.

You also need to make some formatting decisions. How would you like to record a video and when would you like to air it? For example, if you use the Facebook application on iOS, you can place the video horizontally or vertically as needed. Do a test video to see which feature works best for you.

Time is crucial when it comes to videos on Facebook. Send regular email alerts, notifications, or post information about an upcoming event. Your goal is to reach and attract your audience. If you plan a live event rather late at night or early in the morning, you will miss your viewers.

You must constantly offer the audience context. You may think it is enough to introduce yourself or your brand at the beginning of the video and then stop it. Do not assume that the video stream will remain in place as soon as the viewer clicks on the video stream in real time. Also, there may be other viewers who opt for later participation. To attract all viewers, you must periodically provide a context for the video.

The video has to be approachable. Live comments and reactions make the experience more interactive for the user. So, you must try your best to make the user feel like it is a two-way conversation. For the conversation to be interesting, you need to interact with the audience and respond to their comments or reactions.

You can also use this feature to announce any shout outs.

Conclusion

Social media marketing is certainly a buzzword these days and rightly so. The various benefits of social media marketing outweigh the benefits of any conventional marketing methods such as newspapers, billboards, or TV commercials. Of all the various social networking sites available these days, Facebook is considered to be the best platform for social media marketing. With over a billion active global users on Facebook, it is quite likely that you will certainly find your target audience. Facebook has great potential, and its popularity seems to be increasing every day.

By understanding how you can make the most of this wonderful platform, you can create a marketing strategy that will help you attain your business objective. In this world dominated by social media, businesses can no longer afford to lag. Time, effort, and patience are the cornerstones for developing a successful Facebook marketing strategy!

In this book, you were given all the information you need about Facebook marketing and the various steps you can follow to create an effective marketing strategy that will help target your ideal audience. Carefully go through all the information given in this book and keep it in mind while developing a marketing strategy. You will certainly see positive results if you do it properly.

Now, all that's left for you to do is start using the information given in this book to design a perfect marketing strategy for your Facebook account. Take the first step and get started with Facebook marketing as soon as you can to reap all the benefits it offers.

I want to thank you for purchasing this book. I hope it proved to be an informative and engaging read. Good luck on your journey to master the art of Facebook marketing!

References

4 Tips for Planning Your 2019 Facebook Marketing Strategy. (2019). Retrieved from https://medium.com/@the_manifest/4-tips-for-planning-your-2019-facebook-marketing-strategy-411a70de7936

7 Facebook Stories Best Practices for Business Owners. (2019). Retrieved from https://curatti.com/facebook-stories-best-practices/

10 Common Facebook Marketing Mistakes (and How to Avoid Them) - dummies. (2019). Retrieved from https://www.dummies.com/business/marketing/social-media-marketing/10-common-facebook-marketing-mistakes-and-how-to-avoid-them/

10 Tips for Creating Content on Facebook That Gets the Thumbs Up. (2019). Retrieved from https://www.wordstream.com/blog/ws/2011/10/19/10-facebook-tips-for-content

16 Effective Facebook Marketing Strategies for Businesses. (2019). Retrieved from https://roelmanarang.com/effective-facebook-marketing-strategy/

The Best Free and Paid Facebook Analytics Tools. (2019). Retrieved from https://www.brandwatch.com/blog/8-free-facebook-analytics-tools/

Cannon, T. (2019). How to Use Facebook Ads Manager: A Guide for Beginners. Retrieved from https://www.socialmediaexaminer.com/facebook-ads-manager-guide-for-beginners/

Enterprise, F., Agencies, F., Business, F., Management, F., Marketing,

F., & Care, F. et al. (2019). 11 Facebook Metrics Every Brand Needs to Track. Retrieved from https://sproutsocial.com/insights/facebook-metrics/

Facebook Ads: The Complete Guide to Getting Started with Facebook Ads. (2019). Retrieved from https://buffer.com/library/facebook-ads

Facebook Analytics Tools: 6 Alternatives to Facebook Insights. (2019). Retrieved from https://www.razorsocial.com/facebook-analytics-tools/

The Facebook Pixel: What It Is and How to Use It. (2019). Retrieved from https://blog.hootsuite.com/facebook-pixel/

How to Create the Perfect Facebook Business Page [Start Guide]. (2019). Retrieved from https://buffer.com/library/how-to-create-manage-facebook-business-page

How to Stop Wasting Your Facebook Ad Budget. (2019). Retrieved from https://www.postplanner.com/blog/how-stop-wasting-facebook-ad-budget/

Hughes, C. (2019). 13 Facebook Analytics Tools to Check Out in 2019. Retrieved from https://blog.iconosquare.com/facebook-analytics-tools-2019/

Soni, A. (2019). Facebook Boost Post: 5 Crucial Tips to Boosting Post on Facebook. Retrieved from https://www.digitalvidya.com/blog/facebook-boost-post/

The Step-by-Step Guide to Creating a Facebook Sales Funnel. (2019). Retrieved from https://neilpatel.com/blog/facebook-sales-funnel/

Svetlik, J. (2019). What is Facebook Stories and how does it work? Retrieved from http://home.bt.com/tech-gadgets/internet/social-media/facebook-stories-what-is-it-and-how-does-it-work-11364169985164

Tomasetti, B. (2019). How to Analyze Your Facebook Ad Results. Retrieved from https://www.smartbugmedia.com/blog/how-to-analyze-facebook-ad-results

Top 25 Benefits of Facebook Advertising & Why Every Business Needs It. (2019). Retrieved from https://www.lyfemarketing.com/blog/facebook-advertising-benefits/

Trends, S., Users, H., & Bose, S. (2019). Have You Seen This List of Resources for Facebook Business Users? - Small Business Trends. Retrieved from https://smallbiztrends.com/2015/12/facebook-business-resources.html

Widmer, B. (2019). How to Get Started with Facebook Analytics. Retrieved from https://www.socialmediaexaminer.com/facebook-analytics-how-to-get-started/

Works, H., Agencies, F., e-Commerce, F., Businesses, F., Advertiser, F., & Features, A. et al. (2019). 10 Brain Dead Facebook Ad Mistakes (and How to Fix Them). Retrieved from https://adespresso.com/blog/facebook-ad-mistakes-fix/

Made in the USA
Middletown, DE
26 November 2020

25256016R00186